The Reformed Imperative

The Reformed Imperative

What the Church Has to Say That No One Else Can Say

John H. Leith

The Westminster Press
Philadelphia

Book design by Gene Harris

First edition

Published by The Westminster Press®
Philadelphia, Pennsylvania

PRINTED IN THE UNITED STATES OF AMERICA

9 8 7 6 5 4 3 2 1

Library of Congress Cataloging-in-Publication Data

Leith, John H.
   The reformed imperative : what the Church has to say that no one else can say / John H. Leith. — 1st ed.
      p.   cm.
   Bibliography: p.
   ISBN 0-664-25023-8 (pbk.)

   1. Presbyterian Church—Doctrines. 2. Reformed Church—Doctrines. 3. Presbyterian Church (U.S.A.)—Doctrines. I. Title.
BX9175.2.L45 1988
230'.5—dc19   87-30879
                                                                      CIP

For friends
whose friendship has been for me
a means of human grace
and of divine grace

Contents

Foreword

The Reformed Imperative is an apt title for these chapters. It is that for several reasons. First, it catches the author's intention not only to discern salient Reformed convictions that shaped the descendants of John Calvin but also to refresh them by restatement and application. In doing so, Professor Leith provides mandates for the church today, imperatives for faithfulness.

Another feature of these chapters is that Professor Leith infuses familiar doctrines with lively and dynamic interpretations, inviting and encouraging the reader to explore further and to think imaginatively. The past becomes an entrance into contemporary reflection about the present and future shape of Christian belief.

Finally, in these chapters, the imperatives of the Reformed faith—the claims made upon the individual Christian and Reformed churches today—are lodged firmly in the indicatives of God's gracious gifts. The priority of God's initiative is held high in good Reformed fashion and then joined by reflections on the human response. The Reformed logic is maintained.

These chapters were, in substance, originally given as the Thomas White Currie Lectures at Austin Presbyterian Theological Seminary. These lectures were established and are funded by the Tom Currie Bible Class of the Highland Park Presbyterian Church in Dallas, a class taught weekly by the late Dr. Currie when he was simultaneously president of Austin Presbyterian Theological Seminary and interim pastor of the Highland Park Church. Dr. Currie's arduous commuting each week between Austin and Dallas, Texas, in order to fulfill both responsibilities was a symbol of his conviction of the need for intimate and dynamic interaction between the seminary as the academy of the church and the church as congregation. Professor Leith in these chapters also represents that interaction. In doing so, he fulfills nobly the heritage of the Currie Lectures.

JACK L. STOTTS

Austin Presbyterian Theological Seminary   *President*

Preface

The occasion for this book was the invitation of the faculty of Austin Presbyterian Theological Seminary to give the Thomas White Currie Lectures in February 1987. The lectures are funded by the Currie Bible Class of the Highland Park Presbyterian Church in Dallas in honor of Thomas W. Currie (1879–1943), who was interim pastor of the Highland Park Church from 1932 to 1937, and who served as president of Austin Presbyterian Theological Seminary from 1922 to 1943. Thomas W. Currie was a great preacher and churchman whose ministry has been carried on by three sons, who are all Presbyterian ministers, and a daughter who was actively involved in the official work of the church. The tradition continues through the ministries of his grandsons, James S. Currie and Thomas W. Currie III; I came to know the latter at the University of Edinburgh as he was writing his dissertation on Karl Barth. The fact that these lectures are in honor of Thomas W. Currie strongly suggested that they should have to do with the proclamation of the gospel in the life of the church. The lectures were given in the hope that they would contribute to the tradition of preaching, teaching, and pastoral care which he so ably represented.

The theme suggested by the life and work of Thomas W. Currie has to be set today in the context of the decline of mainline Protestant churches and in particular the radical decline of the Presbyterian Church as a factor in American religious life during the past two decades. The quantifiable facts indicating the decline of the Presbyterian Church (U.S.A.) are numerous and varied. The church has had a net loss, in the twenty years 1966–1986, of 1,233,277 members. Congregations have declined by 1,406, though approximately 250 new Korean congregations have been organized. The decline in church school membership has been over 52 percent. The loss in male members is significant, dropping from 50.56 percent of total membership in 1976 to 40.63 percent in 1986.[1] The church is increasingly older and has fewer younger people. According to the Gallup Organization the percentage of the population declaring a Presbyterian preference has declined from six out of a hundred in 1967 to four out of a hundred in 1982.[2] Polls also indicate that Presbyterian church attendance in the period has dropped from 37 percent to 28 percent. In the same period Baptist attendance increased from 38 percent to 41 percent.[3] While Presbyterian membership and participation were declining, the population of the United States was increasing from 196,560,000 to 238,816,000 in 1985.

The Presbyterian Church in the past has influenced American society out of proportion to its numerical membership. It has been an overwhelmingly middle-class and professional church, a characteristic that has been true since the time of the Reformation. There are indications that the Presbyterian Church is becoming less middle-class and less professional, particularly in relation to other churches in our society, churches which in the past have had few middle-class and professional persons in their membership.

The decline in church membership and attendance indicates that Presbyterians will have less and less influence upon economic, political, and social issues in the public sector. The present role of Presbyterians in public life is based on the strength of the church twenty-five years ago. *Forbes* magazine, in a survey of the executives of the hundred largest corporations, found that 25 percent of their respondents were Presbyterians.[4] The question that faces us is the prospect for Presbyterian influence in the future. The quantifiable statistics all indicate that the public influence of Presbyterians will diminish.

The activity of Presbyterians in political life presents a strange anomaly. Never before have the Presbyterian General Assemblies and the various staffs of the church been so prolific in turning out political, social, and economic pronouncements and in the funding of political advocacy organizations. This political activity has generally been in agreement with the political positions of the left wing of the Democratic Party. Yet the last significant political action in which Presbyterians engaged was the election of Ronald Reagan. The surveys indicate that Presbyterians voted 68 percent or more for Ronald Reagan, an unusual consensus in a large organization.[5]

Politicians do not listen to the official pronouncements of the church when they know that attendance in local congregations is declining and, moreover, when they also know that the actual membership of the church will not in their political activities support the church's official positions. In a large measure, the political pronouncements of the Presbyterian Church have become sound and fury, signifying little. Church staffs and committees may organize a Washington lobby or form a network to write letters and send telegrams to members of Congress, but the church seems to have less and less influence on economic, social, and political life. In fact, there is considerable evidence that Presbyterians in Congress, who are in many cases very active church people, pay little attention to the actions of the General Assembly and to the church's staff. In the 1950s and 1960s the Presbyterian Church still had grassroots strength and the integrity of a tradition that gave force to its political concerns. But today that capital seems to have been used up. This decline in the Presbyterian Church's influence on the political life of the country is parallel to a rise in the influence of the conservative churches.

Many factors have no doubt contributed to the declining role of the Presbyterian Church in American life, along with the declining role of other mainline Protestant denominations. This book is written, however, in the conviction that the primary source of the decline is to be found in the loss of the theological integrity and competence of the church's witness, in particular in preaching, teaching, and pastoral care. There was a time when Presbyterian preaching reflected the highest levels of competence in society. Can we today claim that in terms of competence our Presbyterian preaching matches the performance of the best professional people in the community in the discharge of their duties—that is, the best lawyers and the best doctors? There was a time when Presbyterian preaching brought to bear on individual and public life the wisdom of the classical sources of theology: namely, the Bible, the theology of the ancient Catholic church, and of classical Protestantism. The faith that was believed and confessed was related to the whole range of human experience. Can we really say that preaching today has its roots in this ancient tradition and speaks persuasively out of a knowledge of the Christian faith? Persons in public life will not listen to church people on political, social, and economic matters unless they are first convinced that ministers and church people are scholars in biblical studies and theologians of excellence. Credibility in theological work is a precondition not only for the spiritual life of the church but for respect for the church's witness in society.

The renewal of the church will not come without the recovery of the authenticity and theological integrity of the church's message and a renewed emphasis on preaching. The form of preaching is important, but the first concern of a Reformed Christian must always be content. Without content, form has no substance. It may be good entertainment, but it is not preaching in the great tradition. Moreover, the message determines the form, and in a large measure the message is the medium. Christians believe that the most important event in the history of the human race was the life, death, and resurrection of Jesus Christ, and that the greatest service which can be rendered to the human race is the explication of what God did for our salvation in Jesus and the application of that message to human life in general.

Any wisdom the church may have in matters of political, economic, and social concern, or in therapy, is derivative. It grows out of biblical and theological wisdom as well as out of commitment to the God and Father of our Lord Jesus Christ. Otherwise, the church's political and social pronouncements become cut flowers, severed from their roots. When theological commitment and theological competence are not the basis of the church's witness, the church becomes a back door into politics or therapy, for example, enabling church people to avoid the disciplines of their public counterparts. The use of the apparatus of the church to further political and ideological concerns by those who do not participate in the routine activities of the political parties is subversive both of the political process and of the Christian witness itself. Practical political wisdom is certified by the voters and by performance in office, and professional wisdom in the science of politics may be certified by the best university graduate schools. The only contribution that the church in its official life has to bring to political, economic, and social processes is commitment to the Christian faith and competence in biblical and theological studies which may illuminate political and social and economic life.

The credibility of the church's wisdom in any field depends on the credibility of the faith commitment and on the theological wisdom that is evident in the church's life. Hence the renewal of theology and of theological preaching is not only the human basis for the renewal of the life of the church itself but the basis for the renewal of the church's public witness. Respect for the church's faith commitment and for the theological competence and integrity of its preaching is the basis of respect for the church's message to the world.

Presbyterians have always emphasized the life of the mind as a service of God. Presbyterian sermons have been distinguished by their content. Indeed, the clarity and intellectual perception of the best sermons elicited affections of the heart from those who were enabled to see what they had not seen and to understand what they had not understood. This preaching had its own distinctive emotional force. The Presbyterian way of being Christian was in considerable measure established by this preaching. This is not the only way of being Christian, and there is no best way. But Presbyterianism has been an authentic and powerful way that has been a means of grace to many people, some of whom would not have responded to other ways. Without a recovery of this great tradition, Presbyterianism either will not survive or will change its character. More significantly, the one holy catholic apostolic church will be impoverished by this loss.

The purpose of this book is to contribute to the revival of theological preaching and the proclamation of the Christian gospel, on which every other Christian witness is dependent. The first chapter sets forth the theological and practical significance of preaching, as well as the theological processes that inform good preaching. The remaining six chapters explicate, in a manner one hopes is meaningful for human experience today, six dimensions of the Christian gospel. While these chapters do not set out to define either the essence or the identity of Christianity, they do intend to explicate dimensions of the gospel from which all other Christian witnesses are derivative. The author has been a Presbyterian all his life, but the intention in these six chapters is to explicate the faith of the holy catholic church, albeit with certain Presbyterian overtones.

Many readers will recognize the author's indebtedness throughout to the works of Augustine, Luther's great writings of 1520, Calvin's *Institutes of the Christian Religion,* and the Westminster Assembly documents, as well as to the writings of such contemporary theologians as William Temple, H. Richard Niebuhr, Reinhold Niebuhr, Emil Brunner, and Karl Barth. Among many great teachers, no one has influenced me more than Professor Albert C. Outler. He was in many ways the best teacher I ever had. He is also my friend. He tried to teach me that the first task of any theologian is to be a competent interpreter of the tradition in the idiom of one's own time and place; and that "narcissistic delight in being different and lust for novelty" were enemies of good theology. He also taught me the importance of the law of minimal theological development, as advocated by the theologians of the ecumenical councils and as practiced by John Calvin.

Colleagues on the faculty of Union Theological Seminary in Virginia have always been willing to answer my questions, especially James L. Mays, Paul Achtemeier, Jack Kingsbury, and John Newton Thomas. Professor George Stroup of Columbia Theological Seminary read the manuscript and provided not only the encouragement of a friend but many constructive criticisms.

Theological work owes a great deal to students as well as to teachers. I was fortunate during the time when this book was being written to have some of the ablest students I have ever taught. Some have contributed specifically to this work. Stacy Johnson has worked with me as an assistant, reading and rereading the manuscript. Portions have also been read by William Seel, Ernest Thompson, Alexander Evans, and Laura Hollandsworth Jernigan. They along with others have helped me by their comments and they have encouraged me not only by their own theological development but by their commitment to be preachers in the great tradition of classical Christianity.

One of the joys of theological work at Union Theological Seminary is a library great in holdings and service. Martha Aycock, for many years reference librarian and now associate librarian, has always brought to her work a high sense of vocation and indefatigable energy. Her personal interest in the writing of these lectures has not only contributed to their worth but made the writing easier and more pleasant. The manuscript was ably typed and put into finished form by Sally Hicks.

Working with The Westminster Press has been a pleasant as well as a helpful experience. Keith Crim has been personally interested in making this a good book from the beginning, and his very considerable skills as a scholar and editor have enhanced its quality.

Special thanks must go to those who listened to the lectures and who made the giving of them a good experience that is now a good memory. Jack Stotts, president of Austin Presbyterian Theological Seminary, always thought of my needs in advance. Virginia Stotts contributed not only to my welcome but to the welcome of all who were present. Dean Robert Shelton was my specific host, whose work for my physical comfort was exceeded only by his willingness to engage in theological and ecclesiastical discussions.

The lectures were also given in part in April 1987 as the R. L. Robinson Lectures for the sesquicentennial celebration of Erskine Theological Seminary. Dean Randolph Ruble was as always my thoughtful and gracious host and friend.

This book is dedicated to friends whose lives have been a means of human grace and of divine grace to me, and without whom this book would really not be possible. The communion of the saints is the greatest human reality. Friends as well as personal and spiritual experiences are private, and their names ought not to be made public. Dietrich Bonhoeffer was surely right in insisting that privacy is necessary for the integrity of personality. Yet two of the friends to whom this book is dedicated have meant very much to me, and from their lives I have learned in great measure what it is to be Christian. Henrietta Worsley Davis demonstrated to me not only the wonder of friendship but also the power of the human will to believe when the resources of the heart may be troubled, and the power of the human spirit to live when physical conditions grow weak. Neil O. Davis, my friend for forty years, is by every criterion I know a modern person. A Nieman Fellow in journalism, the founder, publisher, and editor of the *Auburn Bulletin,* he has lived his life in the economic, social, and political world. He and his newspaper made a difference for human dignity and human opportunity in his community and in the state of Alabama. For twenty years he has guided the Presbyterian Community Ministry in Auburn, one of the finest diaconal services I know anywhere. His life has, with a rare consistency, embodied the Augustinian dictum "I believe in order to understand" and the Anselmian rubric "Faith seeks understanding."

The best embodiment of theology is not in books but in persons and communities. The best theology is formulated not in the study alone but in community. These lectures owe much of any merit they may have to church and family, to my having been a pastor and a teacher of pastors, and above all to the communion of saints who have supported me and engaged me in the discussion of the issues of life and death in the light of our shared faith.

JOHN H. LEITH

Union Theological Seminary in Virginia
August 1987

The Reformed Imperative

1

Christian Witness Today

The Protestant Reformation was born in the conviction that the church could be revived and reformed by preaching "the most holy gospel of the glory and grace of God," the true treasure of the church.[1] The first thesis of Berne (1528) declared "the holy Christian Church, whose only Head is Christ, is born of the Word of God, and abides in the same, and listens not to the voice of a stranger."[2] John Calvin (1509–1564) and other Reformed pastors had no program for the church other than preaching and teaching the Word of God, administering the sacraments, and providing pastoral care. The church lives, they believed, by hearing the Word of God.

Today the churches of the Reformation are in a period of crisis. The decline of Reformation churches in western Europe has occurred in the context of secular humanism and even the rise of neopaganism.[3] It has taken place in the United States, however, while the Christian community is growing at least as fast as the population, and side by side with Christian revivals. In fact approximately 90 percent of the American people claim some religious identity, and 40 percent attend church services to worship God each week. Furthermore, many congregations in declining denominations, not always in good locations, have all the signs of spiritual life and theological vigor, as well as numerical growth. The culture may in many ways be increasingly secular, but the possibility of the renewal of the church is evident.

In recent years the so-called mainline churches have sought to stem the decline with better management and emphasis on processes, with liturgical reform, with reorganization, and at times with an obsessive desire to become relevant. None of these strategies has been successful.

Many factors have contributed to the malaise of the church. The general secularism of the culture, in which life is increasingly lived as if there were no God, is a factor. Of equal significance is the new social situation in which there is little support for the church in the general structures of society. We have moved from the parish church in Christendom or Protestantdom to the highly voluntary church in a free, pluralistic, mobile, mass-media-dominated society. The pluralism of society in particular undermines the sense of identity that was given to an older generation by birth, church, and community.

The plight of the church cannot be explained away in terms of the social environment. There is abundant evidence that wherever there is good preaching, good teaching, and good pastoral care which incorporates people into the life of the church, congregations thrive. The decline in preaching is closely related to the decline in membership. This deterioration of preaching is twofold, first a decline in homiletical skills and labor, and second a decline in theological and biblical content. Careful attention to sermon craft, and especially to delivery, is not as apparent as it was in a generation that lived under the shadow of Harry Emerson Fosdick. While form without content is fraudulent and corrupting, preaching worthy of the message, as Calvin wrote Protector Somerset (October 22, 1548), must be "lively."

The primary source of the malaise of the church, however, is the loss of a distinctive Christian message and of the theological and biblical competence that made its preaching effective. Sermons fail to mediate the presence and grace of God. Many sermons are moral exhortations, which can be heard delivered with greater skill at the Rotary or Kiwanis Club. Many sermons are political and economic judgments on society, which have been presented with greater wisdom and passion at political conventions. Many sermons offer personal therapies, which can be better provided by well-trained psychiatrists. The only skill the preacher has—or the church, for that matter—which is not found with greater excellence somewhere else, is theology, in particular the skill to interpret and apply the Word of God in sermon, teaching, and pastoral care. This is the great service which the minister and the church can render the world. Why should anyone come to church for what can be better found somewhere else?

The secularization of the church, and especially the demand that the church be relevant to an increasingly secular society, has confused the theological task of the church, and preaching in particular. In a secularized church, theology frequently becomes the effort of rational people to discover a credible God.[4] In a secularized church, ethics becomes the endeavor of political activists to find a relevant prophetic message to be pronounced in the name of the transcendent God. This is a reversal of the ancient tradition. The result is that there is little difference between what the church has to say and what we hear from therapists, from political advocates, and from the various political parties. Augustine believed that faith and love were necessary for theology and for ethical reflection. He and the Reformers after him insisted that in all theological and ethical reflection priority must be given to revelation, to faith, to life in the worshiping, believing community. "We believe in order to understand." "Faith seeks understanding." Faith does not seek demonstration, but it does seek intelligibility, the intelligibility of the faith itself and of human existence in the world in the light of that faith. This is the intellectual task of preaching.

Preaching is more than an intellectual task. It is also the proclamation of the gospel, calling the sinner to repentance and to faith. It is a means of grace to heal, comfort, and give hope to persons whose consciences have been wounded and whose spirits have been bruised. Preaching is an incredibly presumptuous task, as it is uttering words that by the power of the Spirit become the words of God who is our Creator, Judge, and Redeemer. Preaching is possible only as the preacher is identified with all who hear. The renewal of the church will come with the recovery of the sermon that is not moral advice or political rhetoric or personal therapy or entertainment but the means of God's grace to forgive and to sanctify, to heal and to fortify human hearts for the great crises and challenges of life.

The emotional, persuasive power of the sermon arises primarily out of the message. Attention has to be given to form, but style must uncover the reality of the message, not enhance it or decorate it. This is what Calvin meant by simplicity. Reason and emotion ought not to be in contradiction. Rational clarity, the reality of discourse that lays bare truth, the beauty of thought following thought and of words being in place elicit an aesthetic experience and deep emotion. Moreover, preaching that uncovers the reality of the gospel and of actual life in the light of the gospel is never boring. Preaching does not have to be a performance, or entertainment, or rhetorical decoration to command attention. Preaching that has the quality of reality builds up congregations and endures, whereas rhetoric without substance fades as a cut flower.

The church in the past has generally been revived by great preaching, especially when preaching has been united with teaching and pastoral care. The Reformation, the Puritan Revolution, and the frontier revivals, events that powerfully shaped American life and society, are all instances of the power of preaching as a means of God's grace. There is good reason to believe that the future of the church in our society again depends, humanly speaking, on the

Christian witness to the world, especially as that witness is institutionalized in preaching united with teaching and pastoral care.

Preaching and the Reformed Tradition

John Calvin understood and intended the Reformation to be the evangelization of the church: that is, the simplification of theology, of preaching, of the sacraments, and of the government of the church, so that the grace of God could be mediated through them to the people.[5] On the human level, the origin of the Reformation is to be found primarily in the bruised spirits and the wounded consciences of people, and in the inability of the structures of medieval Catholicism to mediate the grace of God to human beings in anguish of spirit or in quest of life's meaning.[6] The corruption of the medieval church was a secondary issue. Luther would go so far as to say that the papists might be better people than the Protestants. The central issue was the church's witness.

Martin Luther (1483–1546) and John Calvin, after him, were fully convinced that the basic human problem was not political, economic, or social but theological. Hence they insisted upon giving a theological answer to the human problem and steadfastly refused to allow the theological message to be identified with any human cause. The Marxists have never forgiven Martin Luther his refusal to allow either himself or his preaching or his movement to become identified with the cause of the peasants.[7] The Protestant Reformation, paradoxically, mightily influenced and shaped political, economic, and social life. This influence, however, was a by-product of preaching what the Reformers perceived to be the Christian gospel and of the ordinary life of the church. It is undoubtedly true that economic and political factors did influence the thinking of the Reformers and the subsequent course of Reformed history. But insofar as they were able, Luther and Calvin sought to explicate the gospel in preaching, teaching, and pastoral care.

The Reformation can best be understood as a revival of preaching, the principal means by which God's grace was mediated to human beings. The Tetrapolitan Confession of 1530 titled its first chapter "Of the Subject-Matter of Sermons," in which it declared that in this moment of crisis we "enjoined our preachers to teach from the pulpit nothing else than is contained in the Holy Scriptures or hath sure ground therein."[8] The most decisive statement of the role of preaching is found in the Second Helvetic Confession (1566):

> The preaching of the Word of God is the Word of God. Wherefore when this Word of God is now preached in the church by preachers lawfully

called, we believe that the very Word of God is proclaimed, and received by the faithful; and that neither any other Word of God is to be invented nor is to be expected from heaven: and that now the Word itself which is preached is to be regarded, not the minister that preaches; for even if he be evil and a sinner, nevertheless the Word of God remains still true and good.[9]

A century later, the Westminster Shorter Catechism (1647) declared, "The Spirit of God makes the reading, but especially the preaching, of the Word an effectual means of convincing and converting sinners, and of building them up in holiness and comfort, through faith unto salvation."[10] No clearer statement of the significance of preaching can be found. Protestantism, and the Reformed type of Protestantism in particular, depended primarily upon preaching to accomplish what the whole sacramental system of medieval Catholicism was failing to do in the sixteenth century: namely, to communicate God's grace to human beings.

The revival of preaching at the time of the Reformation was remarkably effective. It delayed the secularization of Europe for at least two centuries. It once again made the worship of God the concern not only of kings and princes but of ordinary people. It established congregations of worshiping people. Preaching brought healing to human souls and was the primary means by which the Holy Spirit constituted the local congregation.

This preaching was the exposition and application of the Word of God and sought to give a theological answer to the human problem. Yet it also mightily influenced society. It became a powerful ingredient in the development of political institutions and in the achievement of enormous economic productivity in northern Europe and the United States. There is simply no way to understand either American churches or American society independently of the preaching of John Calvin in Geneva, of the Puritans in England, of John Wesley (1703–1791) in the eighteenth century, and of those preachers who gave leadership in the establishment of voluntary churches in a free land and on the rugged frontiers of American life. This preaching shaped personalities and society so that tens of millions of people are different personalities from what they would have been, and American society is different from the society it would have been if it had not been so mightily influenced by this tradition of Protestant preaching.[11]

Critics rightly deplore the deteriorating quantifiable dimensions of mainline church life in America today, but it is still very significant that in every part of America millions of people leave their homes, their rest, their recreation, or their work to come to a church building on Sunday morning to worship God and hear a sermon. This is a phenomenon that cannot be duplicated in our society. It surpasses anything that happens in sports, in politics, or in education. It is worth pondering that within a twenty-five-mile radius of almost every stadium where 80,000 to 100,000 gather to see a college football game on Saturday, more people gather on Sunday to worship God and to hear a sermon. All those who would influence human society would give anything to possess what is available to the church each Sunday morning.

Herbert Butterfield, a distinguished modern historian, has put the matter of preaching in historical perspective.

> The ordinary historian, when he comes, shall we say, to the year 1800, does not think to point out to his readers that in this year, still, as in so many previous years, thousands and thousands of priests and ministers were preaching the Gospel week in and week out, constantly reminding the farmer and the shopkeeper of charity and humility, persuading them to think for a moment about the great issues of life, and inducing them to confess their sins. Yet this was a phenomenon calculated greatly to alter the quality of life and the very texture of human history; and it has been the standing work of the church throughout the ages—even under the worst of popes—here was the light that never went out. And in another respect the church never fails; for, amongst all peoples, whether lettered or unlettered, there have always been those who reached the highest peaks of spiritual life. . . . It is impossible to measure the vast difference that ordinary Christian piety has made to the last two thousand years of Christian history.[12]

Reformed preaching, as practiced by Calvin and the Puritans, had two characteristics that must be noted. First, the Reformed deliberately adopted plain-style preaching.[13] Calvin himself was a master of rhetoric, but his sermons were less rhetorical than his other writings. Reinhold Niebuhr (1892–1971), in his *Leaves from the Notebook of a Tamed Cynic,* notes that he deliberately decided not to be a pretty preacher.[14] Calvin too made such a decision, though so far as is known he did not make note of it. There is a certain carelessness about his preaching, and, as William Bouwsma has commented, his sermons are not examples of eloquence.[15] Calvin spoke in plain language, and he intended the message to be the medium. The power of the message rather than the eloquence of the form was the means of God's grace. Calvin himself emphasized the virtue of simplicity. He abhorred the pretentious, the pompous, the ostentatious, the contrived, and the artificial. He placed great value upon clarity, authenticity, directness. Simplicity for Calvin was close to sincerity. The pretentious and the contrived cover up truth, but the simple uncovers the truth. So it was with Calvin's style. He wanted to write and to speak so that the message came through with its own power and authenticity.

The Puritans, who like Calvin were willing to risk everything on the power of preaching, also deliberately adopted the plain style, inserting homiletical instruction in the plain style in the Westminster Directory for Worship. They believed that this method was appropriate to the gospel, and they also believed that the witness to the faith would make its own impact. It is of significance that John Wesley, whose preaching mightily shaped Christian history, was not himself regarded as a great preacher by many of his contemporaries.[16] Again, for Wesley it was not the style so much as the content, the vision of reality conveyed by his preaching, that gave power to his message.

The second characteristic of Reformed preaching is its close relationship to Christian nurture. Calvinist worship requires a disciplined congregation.[17] The content of the Calvinist sermon is directed toward those who have reflected on the Christian faith. The props and aids to worship have been removed. Discipline, however, not only prepares the congregation to hear the sermon, it also nurtures those who have heard the sermon in living it out in their lives. Albert Outler has noted that one reason Wesley's preaching was so effective is that he related it to the highly disciplined life of an early Methodist congregation.[18] The same was true with Calvin, though Calvin never placed the same emphasis upon methods.

Calvin's emphasis upon preaching was also closely related to his understanding of worship. Central to Calvin's worship was the hearing of the Word of God.[19] The distinction is not between a preaching service and a liturgical service, but between two different understandings of what it is to worship God. The Calvinist congregation participated in the sermon by hearing the Word of God. The significance of hearing as congregational participation ought never to be minimized. It is doubtful if participation in responsive readings or in various litanies is as powerful a determinant of human personality as the hearing of the Word of God authentically exposited in a sermon. The Calvinists believed that hearing was the crucial act in worship, not only hearing the sermon but hearing the promise and words of institution in the sacraments. The tremendous power of the so-called preaching service was evident in its historical consequences. Those who heard the Word of God responded in prayer, in singing, and in affirmation of faith as well as the receiving of the sacraments.

Hughes Old rightly insists that prayer and praise belong alongside sermon and sacrament in the consideration of Reformed worship, as the Westminster Shorter Catechism, Question 88, makes clear. Prayer was the appropriate conclusion of Calvin's sermons. The

Psalms were the prayers of the people. The promises proclaimed in the sermon were signified, confirmed, and sealed in the sacrament. Hence, in emphasizing the decisive role of preaching, care must be taken not to put the sermon, prayer and praise, and the sacraments in opposition to each other. It is appropriate to discuss how they function in Christian life and worship as well as their frequency. The priority of hearing the Word is clear enough in practice, but differences developed in the precise content and order of worship. There is no canonical pattern of Reformed worship.

Many Reformed services, such as those of Guillaume Farel (1489–1565), Ulrich Zwingli (1484–1531) in Zurich, and John Oecolampadius (1482–1531) in Basel, as well as Johannes a Lasco (1499–1560), emphasized preaching, with infrequent communion. Calvin planned ideally for a church service that would combine preaching with the celebration of the Lord's Supper, though he compromised for a preaching service without the Lord's Supper. It is inconceivable that he would have celebrated the Lord's Supper without preaching. It is something of a distortion to speak of Calvin's service as a eucharistic service. There is never any claim that the eucharist took priority over the sermon. Even in the celebration of the sacrament, the decisive moment is hearing the Word of God. Calvin repeatedly spoke of sacraments as appendages or aids to the Word, made necessary by our weakness.

The Authority for Preaching

Christian preaching has deeper roots than the Reformed tradition or its effectiveness in the transformation of individual life and of society. "Jesus came into Galilee, preaching the gospel of God, and saying, 'The time is fulfilled, and the kingdom of God is at hand; repent, and believe in the gospel' " (Mark 1:14–15). The Christian community began with the proclaiming of the gospel, and by the proclaiming of the gospel it continues to be a worshiping, believing community in the world. Martin Luther once said, "The ears alone are the organs of the Christian."[20] In our own day, Karl Barth (1886–1968) has reminded us that the reality and the unity of the church consist in hearing the Word of God.[21]

In the New Testament, faith is closely related to hearing. Paul put it with striking clarity: "Faith comes from what is heard, and what is heard comes by the preaching of Christ" (Rom. 10:17). The Gospels are replete with admonitions to hear. "Every one then who hears these words of mine and does them will be like a wise man who built his house upon the rock" (Matt. 7:24). "My mother and my brothers are those who hear the word of God and do it" (Luke 8:21).

It is worth noting that in the New Testament, hearing takes priority over seeing or feeling or tasting or even thinking. It is the primary way Christian faith is communicated. There is some analogy to this in human experience. The reality of one human self is communicated to another human self not primarily by seeing or feeling or thinking, but through speaking and hearing. The deepest realities of the human heart are expressed when one self speaks to another, and the realities of another self are best known when one self hears the other.

Martin Luther liked to insist that it was preaching which by the power of God called the church into being. The only thing necessary for the existence of the church is the Word of God, which is heard in preaching and through the sacraments. Calvin was convinced that preaching was the will of God for the church. The justification of preaching is not in its effectiveness, not even in its power for edification. It is not a practice for which other practices may be substituted should they prove to be more popular or more useful. Preaching is rooted in the will and the intention of God.[22] The preacher, Calvin dared to say, was the mouth of God.[23]

Calvin knew that preaching would create difficulties and problems. It kills as well as makes alive; it hardens as well as it renews.[24] Calvin was likewise aware that while he preached, many people were frequenting the bars in Geneva, and that some were singing uncouth ditties, parodying the Psalms.[25] Preaching is a witness or a testimony that God wills to be made in this world even if all reject it.

The importance of the Christian witness cannot be overestimated. Origen (c. 185–c. 254), a church father who took martyrdom very seriously and wrote on the subject, suggests that having the witness on your lips is more critical than the faith in your heart. This is in radical contrast to the common notion today that it would be better to believe in your heart than to witness to what is not in your heart. For Origen, the witness took priority over the emotion. "Indeed, I would go so far as to say," he writes, "that it is better to honour God with lips when one's heart is far from God than to honour him with the heart and not to make confession with the mouth unto salvation."[26] This can hardly be labeled hypocrisy when the witness was sealed by persecution or by death. Calvin struggled all of his life with the problem of Nicodemism, a label taken from the name of Nicodemus, who came to Jesus by night. Calvin despaired of those who wanted to believe with their hearts without confessing with their lips.[27]

The church lives by the preaching and the hearing of the Word of God. Everything else in the life of the church is subordinate to this witness. As the church has to have only the Word of God to guarantee its existence, so without the Word of God nothing else in the church program amounts to very much. Karl Barth has, more than anyone else in the twentieth century, emphasized the importance of preaching the Word of God. This is the church's fundamental task, and if it does this task well, Barth was convinced, the proclamation of the Word of God under the power of the Holy Spirit will create its own response. Hence the great emphasis of Barth was the integrity of the witness, not the task of relating the witness to human experience.[28] Barth may overstate his position in insisting that the message alone matters. The church in a secular society has to show increasingly how the faith illuminates experience and history. Yet there is no question that Barth underscored the church's first priority: namely, bearing witness with integrity to Jesus Christ as Lord and Savior.

The Theological Content of Preaching

The Christian church is based on two historical facts and on the testimony of the Holy Spirit.[29] The historical facts and the testimony of the Holy Spirit can be separated only for analysis. They belong together in the one historical event that is the New Testament church. The first fact is the historical reality of Jesus Christ—his life, person, words, and deeds, above all his death and resurrection. Christians are by definition persons for whom God is defined and the meaning of life is explicated by Jesus of Nazareth.

The second historical fact upon which the church is based is the apostolic witness to Jesus Christ as it is attested in the scriptures of the Old and New Testaments. This apostolic witness to Jesus Christ has always been the church's witness to the world. The Christian witness is that the Word became flesh, that Jesus is the Lord, the Christ, the Savior, that he is the power of God unto salvation for those who believe. This is the heart of the church's witness. This witness was made as an affirmation about God based on the historical experience of the revelation of God, as Father, Son, and Holy Spirit. The God who became incarnate in Jesus Christ is the God who created all things and the God who is present to us, testifying in our hearts that Jesus is the Christ. The church has also proclaimed many things that are derivative from this basic witness. In our day, however, when many American churches are in a period of radical decline, it is important to return to the original Christian witness as the source of Christian witness today.

The Christian witness is made possible by the power of the Holy Spirit. The Holy Spirit makes it possible to say that Jesus is the Christ, and in this sense the apostolic witness to Jesus Christ is the work of the Holy Spirit. This witness is not arbitrary. The conviction is appropriate to the fact of Jesus Christ as the disciples knew him. Yet the witness then was never simply a matter of reason, of study, of emotion, any more than is the handing on of the witness today. The witness always involved a personal response, a decision or a leap of faith, which the New Testament attributed to the work of the Holy Spirit, God in the power of his personhood, in the human heart.

Any serious Christian witness immediately raises three questions. The first is the question of integrity and the second the question of truth.[30] The third is the question of power and conviction. How is it that the tradition of God's gracious and redemptive presence in Jesus Christ apprehends us as God's act?

The question of integrity must be asked by the witnessing community itself. Does the Christian witness today authentically represent in our culture the original witness? The traditional Protestant test of integrity has been the Bible. Is the witness biblical? In the light of critical historical study, a more sophisticated way of putting the question is, Does the Christian witness correspond to what is perceived to be the decisive revelation of God, in the light of which all other revelations are to be understood? Yet even so, the biblical question is still decisive, for the Bible is the original and authentic witness, and the biblical canon is the context in which the church decided the witness must be known and understood. The Holy Scripture is, according to the Westminster Confession, "the Word of God written."

The authority of the Bible is acknowledged by all Christians, yet Christians vary in their reading of the scriptures. Protestants, who are distinguished above all others by their emphasis on biblical authority, had to acknowledge that Protestants themselves read scripture in different ways. Hence the task of maintaining the integrity and the catholicity (fullness) of the witness remains. The revelation of the mystery of God is beyond human comprehension. Every Christian witness is a human witness who is limited by space and time, by human wisdom, and by human sin. Thus the first obligation of the church is to establish continually the integrity of its witness. This is a responsibility the church owes to itself and to the world.

Protestants have no infallible teaching office, and for them the test of the validity of a witness is finally the approval of the people of God, the priesthood of believers, over a period of time. This judgment cannot be precise and clear-cut in detail, only relatively correct. For this reason, within Protestantism there developed the notion of denominations, which are by definition bodies of Christian people who believe they are the one holy catholic church, but who do not believe they are the one holy catholic church exhaustively. Human finiteness and sin and the fact that the revelation of God is always beyond the final grasp of any person or community simply means that no theological witness is ever final and complete. Witness to the truth of God is itself a human work. Hence it must be continually revised, corrected, clarified, enlarged.

The Christian witness is on the one hand very simple, the clear proclamation that, in Jesus Christ, God has visited human beings as their Savior and as their Lord. On the other hand, the Christian witness is very complicated, because the full meaning of God's redemption is beyond our grasp and must be related to the complicated facts of life. The Christian witness is not given to us in its fullness from the past. In each generation, the Christian community must rework the Christian witness for itself, through scholarly labor and through reflection on the faith in the context of Christian obedience, prayer, and worship. The Christian witness does not come "ready-made" as a free gift from the Spirit, nor does it come from a simple reading of the scriptures. The gift of the Holy Spirit, the sensitivity of the heart, and the intuition of the mind are essential to the witness, as well as is the labor of the mind.

The Christian witness is established in the memory of the apostolic witness itself and its confession through the centuries. Memory is here used in the sense of the appropriation of the witness of the New Testament and the witness of Christians in subsequent centuries so that this witness is internalized and becomes our own witness, personally and communally, in our own time and situation.

A Christian is one who knows that the witness of the past is his or her own heritage. To be a Christian is to know that Abraham and Isaac and Jacob, Peter and James and John, Mary and Martha and Mary Magdalene, Paul and Priscilla and Lois are our own family; that Augustine (354–430), the great North African theologian, is our father in the faith; that Geneva is our hometown, and that Puritan England is the religious rock from which we were hewn.[31]

Christian witness comes out of the tradition and—also by the power of the Holy Spirit—transmits the tradition, hands on the faith. Preaching and teaching take place in the church, a body composed of the living and the dead. It unites those who hear with those who have heard God's call in the past, through whose lives God has established and reconstituted his people. We know Abraham is our father by assimilating the biblical narrative and committing the story to memory, in particular its names, its dramatic events, its great declarations. The Holy Spirit uses the witness to establish the community of faith.

The shaping of the tradition out of which a believer's witness will come is determined in large measure by one's own history in the church, by one's birth in a particular situation and one's being nurtured in a particular tradition, and by a personal commitment that acknowledges the tradition as one's own. Finally, by the testimony of the Holy Spirit, the witness becomes the witness of the heart in the community of faith.

Every appropriation of the tradition, with its emphases and omissions, reflects the strengths and the weaknesses of a particular way of being Christian, as well as the particular strengths and weaknesses of the individual believer. The appropriation that is the basis for these lectures is only one way of being Christian and Protestant. It has good precedent in Reformed Protestantism, and at its best it has been aware of its tension with the fullness of the tradition. In this construal of the tradition, three emphases are important. The first is the broad biblical base, which must be not only known with the mind but deeply internalized. The second emphasis has two foci: both the classical Catholic theology and the classical Protestant theology as the foundation for contemporary theological discussion. The third characteristic is an insistence that the events of the Enlightenment and the nineteenth century must be taken seriously but not too seriously; that is, the spirit of the Enlightenment and its insistence upon the integrity of the human mind must be a part of the theological task, but the dogmas of the Enlightenment must be seen as time-bound and as subject to criticism as any other dogmas in the history of thought.[32]

The broad base of the tradition is scripture, not simply as studied in the school but more particularly as it has been absorbed in life. For some this means being born into a Christian home and church, so that there is no memory prior to life in the church, no words older than "Now I lay me down to sleep" or "Jesus loves me, this I know," no stories older than the biblical narratives. (For others, scripture comes with the impact and power of a startling discovery.) Northrup Frye, a student of the English literary tradition, has said that the supreme example of myth for the literature of the Western world is the Bible, which "ideally should be taught so early and so thoroughly that it sinks straight to the bottom of the mind, where everything that comes along later can settle on it."[33] If this is true for the literary tradition, how much more is it true for theology?

A cardinal doctrine of the Christian community, and particularly of Protestantism, has been the necessity of a broad biblical base for any Christian proclamation. Fundamentalism, with its doctrine of verbal inerrancy, has sometimes made the biblical base very narrow. Critical studies may also be used to reduce the biblical foundation for theology. Generally the tradition has insisted that only the doctrines that are supported out of a broad range of scripture, and are the sense of scripture, are authoritative in the life of the church. At times this rubric has functioned legally, but at its best it functions not as a legal guide but as a source and criterion out of which all Christian theology must derive.

The second tier in the pyramid is likewise very broad: namely, Catholic Christianity, the Christianity of the creeds: the Apostles' Creed, the Nicene Creed (325–381), the Chalcedonian Definition (451), the doctrine of the Trinity, and the theology of Augustine and Athanasius (c. 296–373). Theological immersion in the broad base of the biblical witness and the somewhat narrower but still broad base of Catholic Christianity is the indispensable ground and source for Christian theologizing in all later periods. The ancient Catholic church was compelled by its own reflections on the faith and by the pressure of an alien culture to give answers to the basic questions of Christian theology: Who is Jesus Christ? How shall we think of God? What does it mean to be a human being in a sinful world? In the providence of God the church had as able theologians as it has ever known. It had the Cappadocians—Gregory of Nyssa (330–395), Gregory of Nazianzus (329–389), and Basil (330–379). It had the schools of theology at Antioch and Alexandria, and it had Athanasius and Augustine. Furthermore, it concentrated its energies on the theological questions with an intensity and catholicity that has never been duplicated.

As one moves from the Bible and Catholic Christianity, the contours of tradition become more difficult to define. Medieval theology played an indispensable role in the development of the tradition itself, and Protestantism can be understood only in terms of this background. Yet in terms of the practical working out of this particular theology, the third tier is classical Protestant theology.

Classical Protestant theology means here in particular the theology of Martin Luther's great writings of 1520: *The Freedom of a Christian, The Babylonian Captivity of the Church, The Address to the German Nobility,* and the *Sermon on Good Works.* It includes the theses, confessions, and early writings of the Swiss theologians, Zwingli's *An Exposition of the Faith* and Calvin's *Institutes of the Christian Religion,* as well as the homilies of the early English Reformation. These are the three broad bases upon which this theology seeks to speak.

After these three classical emphases, the shape of the tradition greatly narrows. The next level is the development of the Reformed and Calvinist way of interpreting the faith. This of course overlaps with classical Protestantism, but it is distinguished from other forms of Protestantism and it had its own distinctive history in the Protestant scholasticism of the seventeenth century. The Protestant scholastics have had a bad press and do not receive credit for being the very able theologians they were. Theologians as diverse as Karl Barth and Paul Tillich (1886–1965) in our own time have said that those who do not appreciate the achievements of Protestant scholasticism do not really understand the theological enterprise.[34] The scholastic theologians took the theology of the preachers who initiated the Protestant Reformation and refined it with precise definitions and with sentences that moved in logical sequence. They gave to Reformed theology an international vocabulary and a form that made it easily teachable. They also faced the demands for a comprehensive statement of the faith, logically coherent, and for the resolution of critical issues which preacher-theologians often neglected.

The fifth tier in the tradition is the restatement of classical biblical, Catholic, and Protestant theology on this side of the Enlightenment and the nineteenth century. The Reformed witness to the faith has received in the twentieth century a new and powerful expression by the "New Reformation" theologians, in particular Karl Barth and Emil Brunner (1899–1966). After a decline of influence from about 1955, this theology is now much alive in the 1980s. It is likely to be one of the few enduring contributions of twentieth-century theology. Its unique contribution was the rejection of both the liberalism of the nineteenth century and fundamentalism, and the clear proclamation of classical Christianity on this side of the Enlightenment.

At this point it is worth noting that theology differs according to the primary vocation of those who write it and according to the context in which they write it. In the history of the tradition, theology has been written by bishops who were also preachers, by monks, by the Protestant preachers, and by school theologians, as in medieval and Protestant scholasticism. In more recent years, theology has been increasingly written by university professors who work in secular universities. Theology has generally been written for the church, but increasingly in recent times theology is written for the academic community and consciously for the public community, which lives by a variety of faiths or with no conscious awareness of faith at all. The vocation of the theologian as well as the audience for which the theologian writes has a significant influence upon the shape of the theology written. Life expectancies of theology vary in the secular university and in the church. Some theologies that thrive for a time in modern secular universities have little or no survival capacity in the worshiping congregation, and the reverse is also true. In this particular discussion, theology is written at least in intention by a preacher within the church for the church.

In its origin, the Enlightenment belongs only in part to the Chris-

tian tradition, but in its impact it marks the most significant cleavage
in the history of Western culture. After the Enlightenment, neither
culture nor theology would ever be the same again.

The immediate impact of the Enlightenment and the intellectual
and cultural developments of the nineteenth century on theology
produced three movements, which we now know as liberalism, the
attempt to accommodate the faith to the new knowledge; fundamentalism, the attempt of the conservative spirit to defy the new knowledge; and the social gospel, an attempt of the Christian community
to apply the Christian gospel to the new situation of an urban and
industrial society. In retrospect, it is clear that liberalism, fundamentalism, and the social gospel, for all their particular strengths and
weaknesses, are no longer live options in the forms in which they
became fixed.

Yet it is clear that theology after the Enlightenment will never be
the same again. It is impossible in our culture to escape the influence
of the Enlightenment. The dogmas of the Enlightenment were in
many instances the denial of Christian faith, as for example the notion that scientific knowledge exhausted truth. The spirit of the Enlightenment, however, contributes to the strength of any theology.
The insistence on freedom of inquiry is in the long run essential to
good theology as well as to the integrity of the human mind. After
the Enlightenment we know better than we have known before that
we cannot believe what we know is not true, that any religion which
requires the sacrifice of the integrity of the human mind is bad
religion. Theology after the Enlightenment must come to terms with
freedom of inquiry, with respect for the facts, with the insistence on
the integrity of the human mind in theological work, with the relevance of Christian faith for concrete human experience. For the
critique of the Enlightenment, theology must be grateful.

The Enlightenment, however, did not mean that the tradition of
Christian theology or the Christian witness had to be repudiated. The
great contribution of Karl Barth was his rejection both of fundamentalism and of liberalism and his restatement of classical Christianity
in full awareness of his culture. Many may argue that Karl Barth and
other New Reformation theologians did not always take with sufficient seriousness the questions that the Enlightenment raised for
theology, but no one can doubt the power with which they restated
classical Christianity, a power to which the strewn wreckage of short-
lived theologies during the past three decades bears abundant witness.

The New Reformation theologians offered the possibility of a critical orthodoxy—orthodox in that it takes seriously the canonical scriptures as the Word of God and the formulation of Christian faith in the

great eras of theological renewal; and critical in that it is a witness which demands the integrity of the human mind as God's gift and relates Christian faith to the facts of human experience today.[35]

Justin Martyr in his *First Apology* (c. 155) declared that Jesus Christ "is the Reason of which every race of man partakes. Those who lived in accordance with Reason are Christians, even though they were called godless."[36] Christian faith can in principie include all truth, for all truth is from God. In this sense Christian faith is open to—indeed, welcomes—modern science, Marx, Freud, Nietzsche, the new awareness of other religions, and the developments of a technological and electronic society. Modern knowledge can enrich and deepen Christian experience and understanding. Yet this is possible only when the Christian community is clear about its own identity and the events which are its origin. Christians since Nicaea have claimed that Jesus is the final revelation. He is final not because God ceases to reveal himself, and not because truth is not to be found elsewhere, but final in the sense that any other revelation or any truth is to be understood in the light of the presence of God in Jesus Christ. This is in part what it means to be Christian: to understand modern scientific, social, and cultural achievements in the light of God's revelation in Jesus Christ, rather than understanding Jesus Christ in the light of modernity. Many of the dogmas prevalent in modern culture, such as the conclusion that all historical events are analogous to others or that God cannot be conceived in personal categories or that God does not work personally in nature or history, preclude the possibility of what the apostolic witness declared about Jesus Christ. The theology expressed in this book is consciously related to the Bible, to classical Catholic theology, and to classical Reformed theology, in that order. To say this another way, theology here intends to be biblical, Christian, and Protestant and Reformed.

This outline of Christian tradition is not intended to be definitive. Those who come out of other traditions and other ways of being Christian will formulate the tradition in different ways. The finiteness of the human mind and the parochialness of human achievements mean that we are safest when we openly acknowledge that our reading of the tradition is not complete, not even catholic. Every particular tradition of Christian faith must remain in tension with the catholicity of *the* tradition. The catholic church contains many traditions, and *the* tradition of catholic theology is safest when the traditions are allowed to live in some freedom. The tradition is Jesus Christ, and the traditions are broken apprehensions of what God has done in Christ for our salvation.

The decisive point about the presentation of the tradition out of which the Christian witness for our time is taken in this particular study is the classical character of the tradition. This is to say, the pyramid cannot be turned upside down.

Contemporary theologies can and do make the broad base the Enlightenment and those theologies which have taken the Enlightenment, its dogmas as well as its spirit and method, with full commitment. Theology then grows out of human experience and the theological wisdom of Enlightenment culture. To this broad base, the classical theology of the Bible, of Catholic theology, and of Protestant theology are related. In other words, the pyramid of tradition as presented earlier is reversed.

It must also be noted that the Christian theologian and witness stands within the tradition and, from the tradition, carries on dialogue with contemporary culture and with contemporary formulations of Christian faith as well. The dialogue is with the world outside the church, but also with the world and with the Enlightenment culture within the church. The cultural criticism of the church is necessary to the vitality of the Christian community. Yet the church's existence is endangered when those within the church speak out of the secular humanism of an Enlightenment culture and seek to relate the faith to the culture. The point here is that the Christian witness stands in the broad base of biblical, Catholic, and Protestant Christianity and out of that tradition engages the world, both within and outside the church, in dialogue. It is this particular stance which distinguishes the church from the proclaimers of other gospels in our society.

The importance of deliberately standing within the tradition when engaged in conversation with and reflection upon modern culture is illustrated in the history of theology since Schleiermacher. The perils of allowing culture to set the agenda for discussion and the criteria for theology are greater even than the refusal by a type of conservatism to carry on any discussion at all. James Turner has recently argued that unbelief resulted in part from the decision of church leaders "to defuse modern threats to the traditional bases of belief by bringing God into line with modernity." The leaders were not wrong in relating their faith to contemporary experience and modern knowledge. They were wrong in forgetting "the transcendence essential to any worthwhile God" and that "the world is not tailored to our measurements."[37]

The contention that Christian faith must accommodate itself to modern knowledge always has to be made with restraint, as it can be tendentious, self-justifying, and premature. Christian communities composed of modern people while maintaining the faith of Nicaea and Chalcedon and of the Reformers continue to thrive. Calvin's *Institutes of the Christian Religion* can still compete with any modern theology in the simplicity, clarity, and persuasiveness with which it states the faith. On the other hand, many theologies, having eagerly sought accommodation to what modern people can believe, have not survived well in Christian congregations. There is no convincing evidence that faith in a God who does not act personally in nature or history is as believable to modern, thinking people as a God who does so act. The historical reliability of the New Testament portrait of Jesus Christ is more persuasive to some historians in other fields and to many thinking people today than to some biblical theologians and historians.[38] No person can rightly believe what is known to be false. To this extent the work of critical historians and theologians is very useful to faith. Yet, within limits, what we believe about the historical reliability of the New Testament portrait of Jesus Christ and God's activity in the world is not determined by reading a book, by a course of study, or by research so much as by the community of faith in which we participate.

To be "modern" is not to be without belief. Countless people, modern by social and intellectual standards, believe that the New Testament gives an authentic account of Jesus Christ and that God, as Creator and Redeemer, acts purposefully in nature and history. The issue is not Christian faith versus modernity but, rather, which faith can best give understanding to modern knowledge. The choice is between engaging modern knowledge and the contemporary world from the perspective of Christian faith or doing so from the perspective of some other faith.

Finally, it must be noted that the tradition is not self-sustaining. It does not live by the work of historians and theologians any more than by church organizations. No historian or theologian can explain how the human life of Jesus is God's self-disclosure and our redemption. Indeed, every preacher must bow in awe before the inexplicable possibility that words of the sermon shall become by the power of the Holy Spirit the Word of God. The handing on of the tradition is first of all the work of the Holy Spirit, who bears witness to Jesus Christ (John 15:26). "The Holy Spirit is God in his self-attestation—God in the power which quickens man to this profitable and living knowledge of his action."[39]

Preaching and Christian Experience

The Christian witness is proclaimed in the context of culture and human experience, especially human experience in the church. This raises the second question of truth corresponding to the first question of integrity. Is the Christian faith true? Does the Christian witness correspond to the facts? Is it a fantasy or a placebo to make the hard facts of life endurable? Is the Christian witness simply a manner of speaking, or does it have the resonance of reality? Sooner or later the question of truth must be faced.

No faith can be proved. We cannot get outside of the mystery that encompasses our existence. For this reason we all, Christians and non-Christians alike, live by faith. We cannot prove the faiths by which we live, and yet we must discriminate among faiths. We must also distinguish faith from credulity.

The final test of the truth of the Christian witness is the testimony of the Holy Spirit in the human heart. The assurance of any faith must be internal. An external authority can determine outer behavior, but it cannot command commitment, loyalty, love, or worship. The Christian witness must be known to be true, just as we know the reality of love, in the depths of human experience. Faith always involves a risk and requires courage. There is always, as Kierkegaard put it, a leap beyond the evidence.

There are, however, subordinate tests that are open to public scrutiny and can be applied by all reasonable people to the faiths they profess. In this way we can as responsible persons in some measure discriminate among faiths and distinguish faith from credulity. The first test is the internal consistency and the coherence of the faith itself. Is the faith self-contradictory? A second test is the adequacy of faith in dealing with universal human crises, such as death and the disparity between what human beings are and what they know they ought to be. A third test is the fruits of faith itself. What kind of person, and what kind of communities, does a particular faith influence and produce? A faith is finally embodied not so much in spoken words, and not so much in written words, but in the living reality of a human life and, in the case of Christian faith, in the life of the Christian community. A fourth test is universality. Does this faith find credence among human beings as human beings under different conditions and in many times and places? A fifth confirmation of faith is the community that shares a common faith and life. It is doubtful if any faith can be maintained by an individual without the support of a believing community. Conceivably, an individual's faith may be true and all others wrong, but there is support in the fact that others confess this faith, that this faith has the ring of reality for them.

A sixth confirmation of faith relates directly to the Christian witness in culture: namely, the power of a faith to illuminate human experience. Long ago, Anselm (c. 1033–1109) said, "Faith seeks understanding." Faith does not seek demonstration or proof but intelligibility, the intelligibility of the faith itself and the intelligibility of the world and human experience in the light of the faith. The claim of Christian faith is that the Christian witness does more justice to the facts, makes more sense out of individual life and human history, and better illuminates human experience than does any other faith.

Analogies to this test of faith in God can be found in the validation of faith in many human activities. It is impossible to prove one's faith that a friend is trustworthy or that a lover's love is genuine. All evidence is susceptible to other interpretations. Faith in the trustworthiness of a friend or in the love of another person is established as that faith makes sense out of one's experience with the friend or the lover. A faith can tolerate some unexplained anomalies, but if too vast a range of experience contradicts faith, it is usually given up. Faiths validate themselves in ordinary experience and in the ultimate commitment of life by illuminating and making sense out of our common experience. Even Job's cry that though God should slay him, yet he would trust him (Job 13:15, KJV) could occur only in a broader context that validated it.

The gospel is a message we could not anticipate, but it is not a totally strange word thrown out of the mystery into our history. The Word of God that breaks into our life in Jesus Christ is the Word of the Creator. The Creator and the Redeemer are one God. We cannot by thinking discover God, but when God chooses to reveal himself, we discover that the revealing God is the God who has created us and made us in the divine image.

The Christian witness not only judges the world but illuminates and fulfills the world. No one has put this better than Reinhold Niebuhr.[40] The public historical revelation of God in Jesus Christ corrects, clarifies, and completes the revelation of God in his creation. Yet the historical revelation is believable because it is the word of the Creator. As Niebuhr puts it, without the revelation in creation, the public historical revelation in Jesus Christ would not be credible, but without the revelation in Jesus Christ, the disclosure of God in his creation would remain diffused, inchoate, and incomplete.

The great disparity between Christian faith and experience in the modern world means that it is not enough to recover the integrity of the message. The message must be proclaimed in such a way as to uncover the human condition to which it is addressed and to elicit the questions for which it is the answer. Witness and preaching face on the one hand the problem of heresy and, on the other, the challenge of paganism. Paganism, with its sacralization of the world and with its emphasis on the intensification of the energies, vitalities, and impulses of life, distracts attention as well as misdirects life. Preaching must enable modern people to see that life's true end, the only end that fulfills life, is the glory of God. The true meaning of life is experienced not in the intensification of its energies or in personal pleasure but in the sanctification of life, which integrates the vitalities of life and the freedom of the human spirit, not toward idols but toward the God who creates, redeems, and sanctifies, who alone is worthy of life.

The task of the Christian witness is on the one hand to proclaim the message with integrity and, on the other hand, to help those who believe to understand how Jesus Christ answers the deepest questions of their lives and illuminates and makes sense of their experience within the church. The Christian witness is both proclamation and explanation. However, it must be underscored that preaching is not moral exhortation, not therapy, certainly not entertainment. It is the very solemn endeavor in a fragile and human way to proclaim the Word of the Creator and of the Redeemer to the people whom God has made and to help those who believe understand their lives in the light of this faith.

Theologians of the church have often attempted in the history of theology to define the identity and the essence of Christian faith.[41] The record of such attempts indicates that the answers to these questions finally elude us. The identity and the essence of the faith are very important, but they defy precise definition.

The heart and substance of the faith can be put very simply, as in the answer of Paul and Silas to the Philippian jailer, who asked, "Men, what must I do to be saved?" and they said, "Believe in the Lord Jesus, and you will be saved, you and your household" (Acts 16:30–31). Or, as Paul put it, "If you confess with your lips that Jesus is Lord and believe in your heart that God raised him from the dead, you will be saved" (Rom. 10:9). No theological explication can ever exhaust the full meaning of these simple Christian confessions, which are at the heart of the faith and which determine both the identity and the essence of the faith as it was proclaimed in the New Testament.[42]

This book is not intended to define either the identity or the essence of Christian faith. The intention is to bear witness to that which lies at the very heart and center of the Christian faith: that is, to its identity and its essence. The Christian faith contains many other dimensions that are not treated here. It is contended, however, that the substance of this book does belong to any integral statement of Christian faith and that it contains the witness which is critically needed in the church today.

2
Mystery and Revelation

Human life is encompassed by mystery. It does not explain itself, and knowing how it works does not make clear why it should work at all. For all of our modern knowledge, human life remains a puzzlement.

The Christian witness is that the mystery has made itself known. "God . . . has revealed himself in his Son Jesus Christ, who is his Word issuing from the silence."[1] Or, as the Fourth Gospel declares, "The Word became flesh and dwelt among us, full of grace and truth" (John 1:14).

Mystery

We know more about the world in which we live today than has ever been known before. There is general agreement that the universe came into existence about 20 billion years ago with a terrific explosion that is beyond our comprehension. Radios and telescopes have picked up the dying remnants of a fireball that filled the universe at the time of the explosion. The fact that we can today detect the noise and fire of the explosion only adds to the wonder. Yet we cannot get beyond the fireball, which apparently destroyed everything that went before. So far as we now understand, we cannot know the forces that created the explosion.[2]

The evolving history of the universe is becoming clearer to us, at least in outline. The earth came into existence about 4.5 billion years ago, and evidence exists of upright walkers and toolmakers about 3.5 million years ago. Human origins are very indistinct, most of the evidence having been destroyed in the passing of time. One anthropologist, who has spent his life trying to recover evidences of human origins in Olduvai Gorge in Africa, contends, "The urge to know what happened is very great, an irresistible inbuilt curiosity about our origins. . . . If we are honest, we have to face the fact that we shall never truly know."[3] The precise details about how human beings came to be and how they developed are likely to be forever closed to us, however interesting the hints of that development may be.

The phenomena of the universe, the phenomena of the human, we cannot in practical life either doubt or escape. We know in the immediacy of consciousness the reality of the world, and we also know the uniqueness of the human self, of the human mind, of the human will, and in particular of the human spirit, with its capacity to transcend and to objectify human existence. Yet the phenomena of the universe and the phenomena of the human are puzzlements. Human existence is bracketed. Like words in a parenthesis, human existence, and the universe itself, depends upon what is outside the parenthesis for its meaning. Within the parenthesis there are only intimations of meaning. The forces that brought the universe and human existence into being appear to be beyond the reach of human inquiry. The knowledge that is within human grasp may tell us a great deal more about what is within the parenthesis. But knowledge of what is beyond the parenthesis is closed to us. This is to say that human life is enclosed in mystery.

The interesting character of being human is the continually receding horizon of human existence. The more we know, the more the horizon recedes. We never reach the end. A receding horizon is different from a missing link. Human knowledge may fill in the gaps of our knowledge and the gaps in our power. Yet the more knowledge and the more power we achieve, the more the horizon recedes. At least this has been our experience thus far, and there is no evidence that it will ever be different. There does not seem to be any escape from the mystery that encompasses us.

Yet mystery is not a word that appeals to many contemporary persons. In the 1960s we were assured by the "death of God" theologians that human life can be lived without religion and without asking the questions that are rooted in the mystery of existence. No longer, we were told, do human beings ask the meaning of life; they simply find its meaning in the living of life. Yet the confidence that the puzzlement of existence could be resolved was undermined by the proclivity of modern people to practice astrology, divination, and even witchcraft. Furthermore, the revival of religion itself became endemic in modern societies.

Mystery must be distinguished, as a number of modern theologians have insisted, from problems and puzzles.[4] Problems are due to ignorance or ineptness. The application of human resources— science, technology, logical analysis—can resolve the problems. Some problems, such as a cure for cancer, are very complex and resistant to human efforts to resolve them. The same is true of problems in the social sphere. In fact, many problems may be so complex that they will never be resolved. The point, however, is not whether or not these problems are solved but that in principle they are solvable. Theoretically they could be solved if only sufficient knowledge and skill were brought to bear upon them. For the past three centuries, persons in the Western world have been amazingly successful in solving problems, from growing crops to curing disease, from overcoming the problems of travel and communication to relieving the inconvenience of heat and cold for physical comfort. This success has been the source of the temptation to believe not only that all problems can be solved, in fact as well as principle, but also that the mystery of life itself can be understood and solved as a problem.

Life can also be understood as a puzzle. A puzzle at first glance has the appearance of mystery. We do not know nor can we immediately imagine how the parts go together. Yet once we discover the clue, the parts all fit together neatly. Any mystery is clarified, and the puzzle becomes a rational pattern. Now, some puzzles may be very resistant to human efforts to solve them, and conceivably some puzzles may never be solved. The important fact, however, is that puzzles are solvable, if only we can discover the clue. They may be frustrating, but they do not in the end elicit awe and wonder.

Mystery is essentially different from a problem or a puzzle. First of all, mystery is not in principle, much less in practice, solvable. It is outside the reach of scientific inquiry. Mystery impinges upon us at the boundary of our existence and at the limits of the powers of the human spirit to transcend itself. But it is never within our grasp.

Mystery may be construed first of all as a presence that encounters us in the depths and at the boundaries of our existence. We experience at the boundaries of our existence the whence or the power from which we come, on which we and all things depend and to which we go; the reality to which we are unconditionally obligated and responsible; the grace that knows us and that forgives us. Calvin's conviction that we know God with the same immediacy as we know the reality of the world or ourselves is rooted in this engagement with the reality that impinges upon us on the boundary of life.[5]

The mystery defies objectification and every effort to grasp it or to get hold of it. For we are encompassed by the mystery and cannot view it as spectators. "A mystery is something in which I am myself involved, and it can therefore only be thought of as a sphere, where the distinction between what is in me and what is before me loses its meaning and its initial validity." Mystery is not what is unknown but "that which cannot be grasped or adequately described."[6]

Gabriel Marcel, whose analysis of existence has construed mystery in this way, has underscored the contrast between mystery and problems. Problems can be objectified. They can be subjected to human scrutiny and review. Mystery defies every technique. Mystery meets us as subject, as presence. It is capable of recognition, and by the same token it can be denied.

The proper responses to mysteries and problems differ. The proper response to problems is study, hard work, the application of techniques and procedures. When problems are solved, any mystery is dissipated. The proper response to mystery, however, is silence, awe, wonder, prayer. The more mystery is recognized, the more mysterious and wondrous it becomes.

There is still a further difference between problems and mysteries. Problems when once solved can be repeatedly solved by those who have learned the formula. Solutions to problems, once they are known, do not call upon inner resources or involve one's personal existence. Recognition of mystery, on the other hand, cannot be repeated at will. It involves being grasped by a presence and all the deeply personal factors that are involved, as, for example, even in the recognition of another person.

Mystery can also be approached from another angle. It is embodied in the ancient question, Why does something exist and not nothing? Marcel's analysis of mystery has been criticized because his account of mystery nowhere raises the question about existence of the world. For him, the ontological mystery is not a cosmological mystery. The ontological mystery is rooted in the person, in the encounter of selves. There is mystery in the encounter of human selves and greater mystery in the encounter of the human self and the Divine Self. It has as its locus some center of value, affection, and concern. The world does not evoke mystery in this personal sense. Yet it elicits mystery in the sense of meaning: Why and for what purpose? Milton Munitz formulates the question thus: Is there a reason for the existence of the world?[7]

Mystery not only encounters us in the fact of the world and our own existence, it also engages us in the transcendence of the human spirit. The human spirit transcends, goes beyond every human achievement. All achievements and knowledge only raise further questions. All acts of love only open up further possibilities of love. The horizons of human existence always recede as we approach them. The whither of the spirit goes beyond anything it can grasp and make an object of its scrutiny.

Ordinary human experiences, when subject to analysis, cannot account for themselves. There is, for example, the pervasive conviction that life is worth living. Where does this conviction come from?

There is also the incredible puzzlement that is rooted in the disparity between what we are and what we ought to be. In a world of cause and effect where does the human self come from, with its power to originate activities with no cause finally but itself, to *intend* to organize the energies and vitalities of life in pursuit of a deliberately chosen goal? How do we explain the powers of self-reflection, of wonder, of freedom?

A secular culture can erode the human sense of wonder and the awareness of mystery. Modern people are sometimes deceived by the power of science to solve problems into believing that it will resolve mysteries. More significantly, the massive growth of the entertainment industry disorders life's priorities and dulls sensitivity to authentic wonder and mystery. One of the great tasks of preaching is to uncover a sense of wonder that points to God and an awareness of the mystery of life that is illuminated by faith.

The simple fact is that we are encompassed by a mystery that no range of modern knowledge can dissipate. Crane Brinton once said that metaphysics is as deeply rooted in human life as is sex. Human beings may repress sex only to find that it comes to expression in strange ways. So human beings may repress metaphysics: that is, the who, what, and why questions of existence. Yet these repressed questions force their human expression in the strange religions, cults, and practices of our time. Metaphysics is more deeply rooted in personal existence than sex or any instinct or vitality of nature.[8]

There is no escape from the mystery of the presence which encounters us at the boundary line of our existence, from the mystery of the question of why there is something, not nothing, and from the mystery of the human spirit and human freedom. These are mysteries that cannot be resolved by hard work or technical skill. Mysteries are illuminated by revelation of the Mystery which is their source, and the proper human response is faith, awe, wonder, worship.

"The Word Became Flesh"

The scriptures from beginning to end have to do with the mystery that encompasses our existence. The Bible opens with the simple affirmation, "In the beginning God created the heavens and the earth." The writer of the Fourth Gospel began his account of Jesus Christ by declaring, "In the beginning was the Word, and the Word was with God, and the Word was God. . . . All things were made through him, and without him was not anything made that was made. . . . And the Word became flesh and dwelt among us, full of grace and truth." Here is the self-disclosure of the Creator in whose will and purpose the universe came to be.

The Epistle to the Hebrews (1:1–4) states this same conviction about the identity of Jesus Christ in a Hebraic way.

> In many and various ways God spoke of old to our fathers by the prophets; but in these last days he has spoken to us by a Son, whom he appointed the heir of all things, through whom also he created the world. He reflects the glory of God and bears the very stamp of his nature, upholding the universe by his word of power. When he had made purification for sins, he sat down at the right hand of the Majesty on high, having become as much superior to angels as the name he has obtained is more excellent than theirs.

The Colossian hymn about Jesus stands over against those who in the thought world of the time wanted to make Jesus one of the powers of the world. For the New Testament Christians the world is created and Jesus Christ stands on the side of the creator.

> He is the image of the invisible God, the first-born of all creation; for in him all things were created, in heaven and on earth, visible and invisible, whether thrones or dominions or principalities or authorities—all things were created through him and for him. He is before all things, and in him all things hold together. He is the head of the body, the church; he is the beginning, the first-born from the dead, that in everything he might be pre-eminent. For in him all the fulness of God was pleased to dwell, and through him to reconcile to himself all things, whether on earth or in heaven, making peace by the blood of his cross.
> (Colossians 1:15–20)

Jesus Christ transmutes the mystery into meaning. In him, the Word, the mind of God, the purpose behind it all, God in his self-expression became embodied in a human life. The foundation of Christian faith is in the simple declaration, "The Word became flesh and dwelt among us, full of grace and truth" (John 1:14).

What do we mean when we say that Jesus Christ is the Word made flesh, or that Jesus Christ is the Son of God, or, more simply, that Jesus Christ is God? The Christian community from the very beginning spoke of Jesus Christ as if he were God. The early Christians called him Lord, Savior, Word, Son of God, Son of man, prophet, priest. All these titles refer to the activity of Jesus Christ, to his relation to his disciples, and to his value or meaning for them. For a long time and in many situations, this language of faith and piety was enough. Through Jesus the disciples knew the reality of God.

Arius, an Alexandrian theologian of the fourth century, changed the question. He did not ask, How is Jesus Christ related to us or what does he mean for us? He asked another question: Who is Jesus Christ? Is he really God? Or is he a creature? Arius's answer to this question was as clear as the question. The Son, or the Word, is a creature. He is the noblest of all creation, the most perfect of all creatures, the firstborn of creatures, but he is still created. He came into existence by the will of the Father. There was a time when he was not.

The question that Arius raised had to be asked, and we should be grateful for the clarity with which he put it. In what sense is Jesus Christ God? The Christians, as well as the Hebrew faith out of which they came, spoke of the one God, the Creator of heaven and earth. What is the relation of Jesus Christ to the Creator? Such questions as these inevitably arose as the Christian community reflected upon the faith. They were also raised by observers from the outside. There was no escape from the question that Arius raised. It forced the church to devote its energies to declaring its own understanding of the nature of the Son or the Word.

The early church gave its answer to Arius's question at the Council of Nicaea (325). The council took a Palestinian creed and inserted in it four phrases that made unmistakably clear the conviction of the Christian community that in Jesus Christ we are confronted by the. very being of God. The decisive phrase declared that Jesus Christ was of the same substance (reality, essence) as the Father. In Jesus Christ we have to do not simply with a great human being and not simply with someone who is like God, but with the reality of God himself. God in his self-expression was embodied in the human life so that all who believed in him could become children of God, knowing him as Creator and Savior and Sanctifier.

The theological significance of Nicaea was clear to those who participated in the debates. Athanasius cogently observed that if Jesus Christ is a creature, even the firstborn of all creatures, his knowledge of God is of the same order as ours and his power to bring salvation is limited to human capacity. Some wanted to modify the declaration of Nicaea that Jesus was of the same reality as God. Possible substitutes were that Jesus is like God, or like God according to the scriptures. Such phrases were open to a variety of meanings. The Nicene theologians were insistent that these alternatives did not clearly state what the New Testament Christians and those who followed them in the faith had experienced in Jesus Christ. Carelessness in theological language at this point endangered the whole experience and life of the Christian community. If Jesus Christ is only like God, we are left with the puzzling question: How much like God? If Jesus Christ is like God, then someone else may come along who is more like God. Those who say Jesus is like God presuppose a prior revelation in the light of which they know whether and how much Jesus is like God. As Paul Tillich wrote, if Athanasius had lost the theological debate, Christian faith would have become just one of the faiths of the empire, and Jesus Christ one mediator among many.[9] It is not without reason that the Roman emperors were generally on the side of those who wanted to modify the faith of Nicaea, which would have relativized the authority of Christ, and that the Barmen Declaration (1934), spoken against National Socialism in Germany, was an emphatic reaffirmation of the Nicene faith.[10]

The church had also said that Jesus Christ is truly man. Having declared that Jesus Christ was God, it now had to say in what sense he is man. After more than three centuries of struggle, the church affirmed, with the same clarity with which it had asserted his divinity, that Jesus Christ was truly man. At the Council of Chalcedon in 451, the church's faith was declared to be that Jesus Christ is God and man in two distinct, separate, undivided and unconfused natures which concur in one acting subject. Critics have always found it easy to point to the inadequacies in the Chalcedonian statement, but after fifteen hundred years no one has yet succeeded in stating the mystery of Jesus Christ as God and man any better.

Chalcedon is the place in the history of Christian thought where the church formulated the apostolic witness to Jesus Christ with careful balance, excluding the ways in which the humanity or the deity has been distorted. It set the boundaries to Christian thought about Jesus. Any Christian affirmation must do justice to the humanity and deity and to the unity of the mystery of the human self and the mystery of the divine self in one subject, one person. Within these boundaries Chalcedon was open to further reflection upon the mystery which is finally beyond our comprehension.

A common criticism has been that Chalcedon used the substance categories of Greek philosophy. The theologians of the fifth century did use the terminology that was familiar to them, but when they spoke of substance they did not mean things or objects. The two natures of Jesus Christ refer to the mystery of the divine self and the mystery of the human self and the conviction that in Jesus Christ the mystery of the divine self concurred with the mystery of the human self in one acting subject.[11] Chalcedon did not mean that two different things became one thing. Furthermore, we see some distant analogy to what they were saying whenever we witness the power of one human person to enter into the life of another person so that this person reflects not only his or her self but also the self that has influenced his or her behavior. At Nicaea and Chalcedon, the church was saying that in Jesus Christ, who is truly, authentically human, the very reality of God is expressed, the very reality of God encounters us.

In recent theology, it has been emphasized that the revelation of God in Jesus Christ is provisional. If the provisional quality of this revelation means that the whole reality of God is not yet disclosed, then this is what theologians of the church have always said. The provisional character of revelation is due to our sin, and also to our created, historical, physical existence. The question must be asked if a created being can ever know God directly. Will the revelation of God always be mediated, indirect? John Calvin liked to say that God in his self-expression was truly present in Jesus Christ but not limited by Jesus Christ. The church was attempting to say that insofar as the reality of God can be expressed in and through a human life, God's reality is expressed in Jesus Christ. It was also attempting to say that no matter how great the glory of God yet to be revealed may be, it is the same glory that we know in Jesus Christ.

The affirmation of the divine presence in Jesus Christ made it necessary for the church to affirm his authentic humanity. It also made it necessary for the church to develop the doctrine of the Trinity. Again, from the days of the New Testament, Christians have spoken of God as the Father, as the Son, and as the Holy Spirit, particularly in the baptismal formula and in the words of the bene-diction: "The grace of the Lord Jesus Christ and the love of God and the fellowship of the Holy Spirit be with you all" (2 Cor. 13:14). The doctrine of the Trinity did not mean there are three Gods, nor did it mean the mathematical absurdity that three and one are the same. In the doctrine of the Trinity, the early church was giving expression to the fact that the one God had apprehended them as Father, Son, and Holy Spirit. God was God in three ways. God was God as the unfathomable ground of existence, as the One who acts for us in our redemption, and as the God who is present with us in power as the Holy Spirit. God is transcendent, creative, and immanent.

The works of creation, redemption, and sanctification are appro-priately related to God as Father, Son, and Holy Spirit. Yet the doc-trine of the Trinity is more profound than saying God is God in three ways. The doctrine is reflection upon the way God has revealed himself, and the Christian community's apprehension of this revela-tion. Christians knew God as the unfathomable source of all things; they knew God's presence in Jesus Christ, in particular his death; they knew God in Christian experience. The doctrine of the Trinity affirms that God is in his own being as God has revealed himself. The generating or sending forth of the Son is the way God is eternally. The Son is derived from the Father but nonetheless God. The Father loves the Son and the Son glorifies the Father. In the death of Christ, the Son experienced forsakenness without being any less God and the Father experienced the loss of the Son. The Holy Spirit proceeds from the Father through the Son but likewise is nonetheless God. God is one but not a mathematical unity, just as in a remote analogy the unity of a human self is personal and not mathematical.

The doctrine of the Trinity is the "attempt to clarify the nature of God who reveals himself in Jesus Christ."[12] The going forth of God in revelation and redemption in Jesus Christ is not an accidental happening. This is who God is, the way God is God in his own being.[13] Thus the doctrine of the Trinity even more than the cross is the unique Christian doctrine, clarifying how the transcendent God is present in his creation, especially in the death of Jesus Christ and in Christian experience without being any less God.

The simple declaration that the Word became flesh called for an elaboration of a doctrine of the person of Christ and a doctrine of God. But for our purposes, the doctrinal questions must not obscure the tremendous affirmation of faith that the Word became flesh. The mind of God, the purpose of the mystery that encompasses us, has been translated into human language. This is the Christian witness and the Christian gospel.

For many modern people, the Word become flesh is foolishness, because it is unnecessary. Human beings by their own wisdom and skill can fulfill life. One of the most pervasive heresies in our society is the notion that human life can be completed by human efforts, and therefore we place incredible demands upon a career, upon a marriage, upon social skills. Or we are told if we cannot fulfill life in our own achievements, we can at least find the fulfillment of human existence in community with other people, communities we feverishly seek to contrive. Finally, in modern culture there is the confidence that human life is no mystery. Modern people no longer ask why we are here and what we are here for. To be modern is to find the meaning of life simply in the living of life. Hence the Christian conviction that the Word became flesh is foolishness because it is unnecessary. The self-sufficiency of many modern people is sustained in part by the entertainment industry, which distracts human attention from the self, and finally by the prevalent use of drugs.

The Word become flesh is not foolishness for modern people simply because it is unnecessary, but also because it is impossible. There is no word to become flesh in any case. Many have become so preoccupied with the powers and vitalities of nature, which can be described in scientific textbooks, that it is no longer conceivable to them that there is any power beyond these vitalities and energies.

For others in our society, the faith that the Word became flesh is a scandal. It was a scandal to many of Jesus' contemporaries because the Christ who came was not the Christ who was expected or desired. Christ may be scandal to people who have messianic hopes, who believe that there are purposes and intentions which give meaning to life and which are fulfilled in history. Many Romans found the meaning of life fulfilled in the organized society of Rome, which was based not upon greed and envy but upon justice and reason. Many Jews looked for a Christ who would fulfill life in terms of the law. So in our time many messianic groups find the meaning of life in their political or social programs. Jesus may be co-opted for these programs, but in the end Jesus becomes a scandal because he is not the fulfillment of life which was expected. The Messiah comes not to fulfill our social, political, or economic programs, or our personal agendas, but to inaugurate the kingdom which is God's intention for human life. The Word become flesh is a scandal to those who do not find in him the messiah they desired or expected.

"The Word became flesh" is also a scandal in an increasingly pluralistic society such as that in which we live. If there is a Word to become flesh, this Word cannot be the only word. The Word become flesh is no full embodiment of the mystery, the same substance as the Father, but only a word that is relative to many other words in our society, one word among many words.

Thus for many people in our society, the Christian affirmation that the Word became flesh is on the one hand foolishness and on the other hand a scandal. Yet this is nothing new. As John put it, "He was in the world, and the world was made through him, yet the world knew him not. He came to his own home, and his own people received him not. But to all who received him, who believed in his name, he gave power to become children of God; who were born, not of blood nor of the will of the flesh nor of the will of man, but of God" (John 1:10–13). Or as Paul declared, Christ crucified is a stumbling block to the Jews and folly to the Greeks (1 Cor. 1:23).

The affirmation that the Word, the mind and purpose of the Creator, became flesh is so stupendous that it cannot be made lightly. The experience of the presence of God in Jesus Christ has been expressed in theological language that results from critical reflection. The question of what actually happened in Jesus Christ must be examined with care. Theologians have referred to this as the Christological question. It was the question that engaged the attention of the theologians of the church from the time of Arius until the eighth century. During these four centuries the church was fortunate to have as theologians many of the most brilliant and able thinkers it has ever known. They subjected the church's claim that God was present in Jesus Christ to rigorous scrutiny. The conclusions they came to as thinkers and as believers are to be found in our classic creeds. No one can say that the Christian church has not subjected what it perceived to be the decisive revelation of God to rigorous and careful scrutiny.

The Christological question must continue to be a part of Christian reflection. Much of what Chalcedon did has received overwhelming approbation in the life of the church. Yet it used the categories and language of another culture than our own. Furthermore, modern knowledge, especially knowledge of what it is to be a self or a person, can illuminate our understanding of the mystery. Finally, our encounter with Jesus Christ in the words of the New Testament and in the worship of the church should enable us better to understand what the New Testament writers and the theologians of Chalcedon were attempting to say. Such reflection should above all deepen our understanding of what we mean when we say, "The Word became flesh."

Those who hear the church's witness have a right to expect the church to be clear about its proclamation concerning Jesus Christ. The church by the same token has the right to expect those who challenge its witness to be open and clear about their faith commitments and worldviews. The Christological question for the Christian has its counterpart for those who reject the Christian witness. What is the human experience or what event is the clue by which they understand human existence and reject the church's witness? What is the nature and significance of this "revelatory" experience or event?

The Christian community knew what it was affirming at Nicaea and Chalcedon. The claim that the Word became flesh made sense of their encounter with Jesus Christ, and it made sense of human experience in the church. Yet Christians of the first or fourth or any other century knew that no one simply on theological advice or by the persuasion of reason ever exclaimed, "The Word became flesh." Only in the power of the Spirit can we say that Jesus is the Christ.

The Meaning of the Incarnation

What does it mean in the actual orientation of life to say that the Word became flesh?

The Word become flesh means, first, that the universe, as well as our own particular existence, has its origin in the will, the intention, and the purpose of God. Older Reformed theologians spoke of the decrees of God, which they defined as God's work of creation, providence, and redemption. The decrees of God no longer belong to ordinary Christian discourse or piety, possibly because of the theological arguments and speculations they provoked. We cannot know the mind of God, and speculative theology and highly rational reflection about God's decrees are not meaningful in contemporary society, with its emphasis upon experience and the practical. However, the doctrine of the decrees stated a very important Christian conviction: namely, that God's purposes lie behind the whole created order.

When understood in this modest sense they are essential to Christian piety.

The ultimate option in the matter of faith is the choice between the faith that the universe is the expression of impersonal powers and forces with no prevision of their end and, on the other hand, the faith that the universe is the expression of purpose, intentionality, and love. These purposes and love are revealed through the life Jesus lived in our midst.

The Word become flesh means that the ultimate Reality upon which all things depend is not only intelligible and intentional, but also love that we know in Jesus. It means that God is best understood according to the analogies of the "self" or "person."[14] Jesus surely thought of God in this way, calling God in simple trust, our Father.

The Word made flesh means, second, that all created things have their meaning in the Word. "All things were made through him, and without him was not anything made that was made" (John 1:3).

The God who created the world is the God whom we know in Jesus Christ. In the Judaic Christian tradition, this meant that the world is good, not evil. To say that the world is good means, on the one hand, that it is consonant with love and, on the other hand, that it is rational, with an intelligible structure. In the Western world we have come to take this for granted. Yet one of the most persistent ideas in the history of the human race is the notion that the world is evil, and that salvation is escape from this world, not life within the world. Jesus Christ means that the God who creates is also the God who redeems. Hence human redemption is not something contrary to creation. Neither is it simply the fulfillment of creation; redemption is the restoration of the created order for the glory of God.

The fact that the Creator is also the Redeemer means not simply that the world is good but also that all created things find their meaning in Jesus Christ. As the letter to the Colossians puts it, "He is before all things, and in him all things hold together" (Col. 1:17). The intelligibility and the love which hold the disparate facts of human experience together, as well as the universe itself, are made known in Jesus Christ.

The Word made flesh means, third, that the power which calls that which was not into being and which raises the dead also reconciles and heals. The Creator is the Redeemer. "To all who received him . . . he gave power to become children of God" (John 1:12). Through him God reconciled the whole universe to himself, "making peace by the blood of his cross" (Col. 1:20).

The Christian message is that a Word has been spoken out of the
mystery which encompasses us, that God in his self-expression became flesh and dwelt among us, full of grace and truth.

Some may say it is not true, but no one can say it is trivial. If it is
true, it is the greatest good news that ever came to human beings on
this planet. Those who heard it for the first time called it news; more
than that, good news. The mystery has been transmuted into meaning. Human existence and the world itself are not meaningless hap-
penings but the expression of purpose, of intentionality, and, above
all, of intelligibility and love, which have been made known in Jesus
Christ.

3
The Power of God
Unto Salvation

The Christian gospel is not simply that a word is spoken out of the silence that encompasses us, it is also "the power of God for salvation to every one who has faith, to the Jew first and also to the Greek" (Rom. 1:16). "To those who are called, both Jews and Greeks, Christ [is] the power of God and the wisdom of God" (1 Cor. 1:24). He not only enlightens our ignorance, he also reconciles us by his atonement and renews us by his Spirit. There is a balm in Gilead to heal the wounded sinner. There is a grace that enables ordinary people to live gracefully amid the crises and challenges of life.

The Need for Salvation

The gospel is the word of Jesus to the paralytic, "My son, your sins are forgiven" (Mark 2:5). Paul put it more theologically. "Therefore, since we are justified by faith, we have peace with God through our Lord Jesus Christ" (Rom. 5:1).

The word "forgiveness" has many usages in our society. For some, forgiveness is a quality of human existence, if not of the universe itself. It is rooted in the general disposition of God, of human beings, and perhaps of the entire order of things. It is popularized in clichés—I'm OK, you're OK. Forgiveness is simply the proper way human beings order themselves, and it is the disposition we have a right to expect from the entire order of existence. In this sense, forgiveness is very simple. It can be claimed without embarrassment and it can be given without cost. W. H. Auden in his *For the Time Being: A Christmas Oratorio* has Herod exclaim, "Every crook will argue: 'I like committing crimes. God likes forgiving them. Really the world is admirably arranged.' "[1]

The Bible, however, nowhere regards forgiveness as simple or as the expression of a general disposition. The question is, rather, Is forgiveness possible? Can history be more than judgment? Does God have a freedom over righteousness that can show mercy without compromising the moral order? The presupposition of the Christian gospel is that forgiveness is never without cost, without the cost of atonement on the part of the forgiver, and without the cost of repentance on the part of the forgiven.

If some in our society view forgiveness as something they have the right to expect in the general living of life, many others find forgiveness unnecessary and even in a fundamental sense undesirable.

The plight of human life is that we cannot save ourselves, even though the achievements of the physical and social sciences have been great. The evidence for our human "lostness" is very convincing in at least four dimensions of life. (1) We are sinners, who sin not only in our worst deeds but in our best deeds, which are flawed by our own self-interest. (2) We cannot guarantee the future even when that future involves us on the deepest personal levels of life. (3) We cannot complete human life by our own efforts. (4) We cannot escape the frustrations and defeats which are rooted in the pathetic, tragic, and ironic dimensions of human life. As created and "fallen" human beings we cannot live either in private or public life with serenity, dignity, and poise apart from the grace of God. Our question is still the question of Jeremiah: "Is there no balm in Gilead?"

Four hundred years ago, Martin Luther was tormented by the question, How shall a sinful person stand in the presence of a righteous God?[2] Using all the means of medieval Catholicism, he sought to guarantee for himself a place in heaven. He became a monk; he confessed his sins; he went on pilgrimages. But he could never guarantee his place in heaven. He could always imagine himself a better monk or a more faithful confessor or a more diligent pilgrim. Today, there are not many people who feel guilty before Almighty God. Our culture, which is very different from that of the sixteenth century, or the first century, precludes such a possibility. But everywhere, in middle-class American society, people feel guilty—guilty that they have not been good parents, guilty that they have not been financially successful, guilty that they have not been socially accepted. Even in the church we feel guilty, or at least the best people do, that the church is not really what it says it is, the people of God.

The fragile character of human existence is nowhere better revealed than in our inability to guarantee the future. None of us knows what the future holds for us or for our world. We do not know what we ourselves shall do under pressure or temptation or even in the midst of apathy. Yet we are under constant pressure to guarantee the future of a marriage, of a job, of financial transactions, of a social revolution. We live in a merit society, where success pays great rewards and failure is frightfully painful. Yet we cannot guarantee the future. There is no assurance in advance that this marriage will turn out as we had hoped, that the race problem will be resolved, that the vision we have of life at twenty will be fulfilled at fifty. This is our predicament. We sing, "We shall overcome," but we may not overcome. What then?

In our secular age, the ancient form of the question experienced in terms of guilt before God is experienced in other ways. We cannot guarantee the future, any more than those who have gone before. We cannot by hard work earn our place in heaven. We cannot complete our lives by our own efforts, nor can we fulfill them by participation in our human communities. Life is not completed in the nation or in economic, social, religious, or therapy groups. The contemporary demand for "support groups" may turn out to be a sign that in the end all groups fail.

Two basic characteristics of all human behavior signify that human life cannot complete itself either by its own efforts or through the support of the various communities to which modern people belong. First, the human spirit has the capacity to go beyond the best we have done. We always know there is something more. Every human achievement opens up new possibilities of further achievement. Every act of love opens up new possibilities of love. Human life has been so created that we cannot exhaust its possibilities in our own achievements or in our communities. There is always something more. This fact about human life is confirmed in the biographies of the most successful. Not infrequently, those who have accomplished the most are most aware of the unfulfilled possibilities of their lives. Human life has been so made that it can only be completed in God. As Augustine put it long ago, "Thou hast made us for thyself and restless is our heart until it comes to rest in thee."[3]

Our problem is not simply that the human spirit goes beyond our highest achievements; it is also that our highest achievements are corrupted by self-love. Martin Luther knew better than anyone else in human history that we sin not simply in our worst deeds, we sin in our best deeds. Or, as Reinhold Niebuhr in our time has taught us, our causes are never as righteous as we think they are, and our participation in them is never as devoid of self-interest as we claim.[4]

This theological judgment of classical Protestantism that we sin in our best deeds as well as our worst is likewise confirmed in the experience of countless good people as they have reflected back over their own lives. No one has said this so perceptively and acutely as T. S. Eliot in "Little Gidding," when he speaks of the "rending pain of re-enactment" as the true character of what we have been and done even in our best moments is exposed.[5]

There are brief moments in life, especially when we are young, when we feel no need for a God who forgives our sins or redeems our life from destruction. Our personal endowments enable us to exult in the freedom of the secular city; our psychological defenses easily convince us of our own righteousness. But these moments are brief. For health breaks; hopes are unfulfilled; the limits of our will-power become painfully clear. Finally we become aware that the achievements in which we invested so much of our lives were possibly not worth the cost, or that our involvement in them is not so noble as once we imagined. Sooner or later we also discover that life is an uphill battle, which in the end every person loses. We know finally that no one ought to underestimate the vicissitudes of life or the precariousness of the human enterprise.

Human life, as Reinhold Niebuhr so astutely pointed out, is pathetic, tragic, ironic.[6] The pathetic and pitiable dimensions of life are seen most vividly in the case of a deformed child or of a human being overwhelmed by forces over which he or she has no control. Other aspects of life are tragic, as when we have to deny one loyalty for the sake of another loyalty, and when we have to do evil for the sake of good, or when the only choices open to us are evil. Some aspects of life are ironic, as when a man's wisdom becomes his undoing because he did not know its limits, or when a woman's strength becomes her downfall because she trusted it too much. The final human predicament is the irony that our finest achievements have human flaws for which we are responsible.

Once we reflect upon the pathetic, the tragic, and the ironic aspects of human life, it becomes clear that we grossly oversimplify life when we make unqualified distinctions between the good people and the bad, between the successful and the failures. One of the great failures of "fundamentalism," in theology as well as in politics, is its inability to recognize the pitiable, the tragic, and the ironic dimensions of human existence. Fundamentalism, in any of its various forms, whether on the left wing or the right wing of the ideological spectrum, makes too simple a distinction between people. On the one hand there are good people who work hard and who have money, who obey the laws and who go to heaven, who are identified with the right causes and make the right pronouncements about society. On the other hand, there are lazy people who do not work hard and who do not have money, who disobey God and who do not go to heaven, who have wrong ideas about the issues of our day. The people who make these distinctions always think of themselves as the hardworking who deserve money, as the good who are going to heaven. There is no gospel in this, only a self-righteousness that is self-deceiving. The gospel is hidden from those who in their self-righteousness cannot see the sorrow and the tragedy in the worst life. The gospel is hidden from those who do not understand that success is not even a possibility for those who have a poor biochemical inheritance or an impossible social environment. The gospel is hidden from those who in their self-righteousness are proud of their moral achievements, who know that they are righteous by their identification with the proper causes, who are vindictive toward the failures, who have only one solution for failures—to discard them, to electrocute them, to destroy them.

There is no gospel for the "righteous." In the New Testament the basic cleavage between human beings is not between rich and poor, the powerful and the oppressed, male and female, the free and the enslaved, but between those who believed they were righteous and those who knew they were sinners. The gospel is for the poor in the biblical sense—that is, for those who know they cannot save themselves, who know their defense is God. As Jesus, who ate with sinners, put it, "Those who are well have no need of a physician, but those who are sick. Go and learn what this means, 'I desire mercy, and not sacrifice.' For I came not to call the righteous, but sinners" (Matt. 9:12–13). Two important truths about life are set forth in these words. First, Jesus could only help those who knew they were sinners. Second, only those who know they are sinners, only those who have received mercy, can show mercy.

The Christian gospel is directed to the sinfulness, the incompleteness, the pathetic, tragic, and ironic dimensions of life. This gospel is the Christian community's witness to the question, Is there a grace which forgives our sins, which gives courage before an unknown future, which enables us to live with poise and dignity in the presence of the pathetic, the tragic, and the ironic, which enables us to accept the incompleteness of our lives with hope?

This Christian gospel is God's salvation, God's good pleasure. It is dependent neither upon our goodness nor upon our achievements. This gospel finds in the New Testament its foundational statement in the simple assertion of Jesus, "My son, your sins are forgiven" (Mark 2:5). This gospel of forgiveness is not the whole of the Christian faith, but everything else presupposes it.

The Work of Jesus Christ

All this salvation is given to us in Jesus Christ. The Christian church has never been able to pull together the various dimensions of God's grace and of God's salvation in Jesus Christ as witnessed to in the New Testament in one coherent statement, as the early church did with the doctrine of the person of Christ or the doctrine of the

Trinity. The Christian community has been content with a variety of motifs through which Christians have attempted to say what it is precisely that Jesus Christ does for them.[7]

Jesus Christ is our teacher, whose revelation of God not only gives us knowledge but insight. Augustine could speak of the life of Christ as moral instruction. The New Testament says, "Have this mind among yourselves, which is yours in Christ Jesus" (Phil. 2:5). Jesus Christ is our example. After washing his disciples' feet, Jesus said, "I have given you an example, that you also should do as I have done to you" (John 13:15). Calvin once wrote, "Let us learn to choose the kind of life that is consistent with the teaching of Christ so that eagerness for gain may not incite us to take up arms in an impious and wicked battle."[8] Or, as Calvin writes in the *Institutes,* Christ has set before us an example, whose pattern we ought to express in our life.[9]

Jesus Christ reveals to us who God is, and who we are. Yet the work of Jesus as teacher is not simply the adding of knowledge that can be propositionally stated, but insight that illuminates the whole of human existence.

Jesus teaches us and becomes our example not so much through propositions we can learn or a fixed pattern we can imitate as through the story of his life. This story speaks to and makes sense of the story of our lives, the joys, frustrations, successes, and defeats we all know. Proclaiming the gospel always involves telling the story of Jesus of Nazareth as this story is given to us in the portraits of the four Gospels. The old hymn—

> I love to tell the story
> Of unseen things above,
> Of Jesus and his glory,
> Of Jesus and his love—

is more than warmhearted evangelical piety. Telling the story in both theology and preaching establishes our identity as Christians. For Jesus is the kingdom. Telling the story is our salvation.

The story of Jesus is concretely the story of his life, as attested in the Gospels. Otherwise, Jesus becomes a symbol for various ideological concerns. The early Christian confession "Jesus is Lord," for example, has no content until informed by the story. Apart from the story it can be filled with alien ideas and made the instrument of human causes.

The story of Jesus is twofold. It is first his life of trust in God, of openness to other human beings, and of keen ability to perceive and to acknowledge reality. He was among the people as a servant and in that way made known the Father. He was honest and at the same time humble in his dependence upon God. His deeds and words were remarkably consistent. The story of Jesus is also what he did. (1) He preached, announcing the nearness of the kingdom of God and calling people to faith and repentance. (2) He taught the will of God. (3) He healed the sick in body and person. (4) He graciously at meals or in homes or in the presence of human need brought people into the presence of God's grace and mercy. (5) He gathered a company of disciples and sent them forth to preach, to teach, to baptize. The disciples first knew Jesus as a very remarkable human being. They followed him and listened to his words. In fear and trembling they accompanied him as he journeyed to Jerusalem and to his death. As witnesses to his resurrection they came to exclaim, "My Lord and my God!" In a similar way through the centuries people have come to Christian faith as they have heard the story of Jesus as told in the Gospels.

Jesus Christ redeems us, ransoms us.[10] Here the symbolism is that Jesus Christ paid the price for our freedom and for our deliverance. When the church used the New Testament metaphor of redemption, of buying back, it was saying something quite fundamental. Even in general human experience, whenever there is deliverance from evil, a price has to be paid to the evil in the situation. Each spring people die in the James River because they venture out too far into the swirling waters. Others are rescued. Yet whenever there is a rescue from potential drowning, a price has to be paid to the evil in the situation. The price may be no more than the gasoline for a helicopter, but it may involve the risk of human life on the part of those who venture out to the rocks to deliver persons from potential death. And whenever there is deliverance from serious evil, even in general human experience, a price has also to be paid, a ransom given to the evil in the situation.

A third motif is that of Christ the victor, who triumphs over sin, death, and the devil.[11] The Christian imagination was very vivid in elaborating the ways in which Jesus Christ won the victory over the principalities and powers. This elaboration makes more vivid the fact that once there lived in human history a human being who was not overcome by evil, but who overcame evil by good. In the life of Jesus, evil could not turn love into hate. Even from the cross, Jesus prayed, "Father, forgive them; for they know not what they do." Furthermore, Jesus Christ is the instance in human history of a human being who could not be destroyed by death. God raised him from the dead.

This triumph of Jesus Christ over sin, death, and the devil was not only a foretoken of God's final salvation, it was also a victory with which believers could identify and in which they could participate. Irenaeus spoke of the work of Christ as recapitulation. Jesus recapitulated in himself the long history of human evolution, undoing what human beings had done to themselves and fulfilling God's intention for them. We appropriate and participate in this recapitulation.

Very frequently in university communities we see a secular counterpart to this participation in a vicarious victory. Persons who have neither the physical abilities nor the inclination to play in college sports yet identify in a way that enables them to participate in the victories and losses of their team. They do not even say the college won or lost; they say "we" won or lost.

Some Christian communities also spoke of the work of Jesus Christ as deification. Jesus Christ became man that we might become God. As 2 Peter expresses it, the work of Jesus Christ is to enable us to participate in the very being of God. For some Christians this has always been an important theme. The fundamental human predicament has been our corruption and our mortality. Jesus Christ unites us with the life-giving energies of God in mystical experience, enabling us to become all that we are capable of being.[12]

Another stream of thought has spoken of Christ as the victim.[13] The Letter to the Hebrews compared Christ to the faultless victim who through his vicarious death assures forgiveness and communion with God (Heb. 10:10ff.). Paul tells us "Christ . . . [became] a curse for us" (Gal. 3:13) or, in Romans 4:25, that Jesus was "raised for our justification." And in Colossians 2:14, we read that God has "canceled the bond which stood against us with its legal demands; this he set aside, nailing it to the cross."

In the history of doctrine, this particular way of understanding the work of Christ found its classic expression in Anselm's *Cur Deus Homo.* Living in the twelfth century, Anselm used the imagery of a feudal society. Sin is a dishonor to God, and satisfaction has to be made or punishment is necessary. Since the injury has been done to God, only God can make an adequate satisfaction. Since man has done the injury, only man can make the satisfaction. Therefore satisfaction can only be achieved by the God-man who in his life rendered perfect obedience to God and who in his death bore our sins. Satisfaction having been made, forgiveness is possible without violence to the moral order.

Anselm's understanding of the work of Jesus Christ has always been subject to caricature and can appear remote from human experience. Yet in actual fact he was saying something that is very significant, and his understanding of the work of Christ is the most profound in the Christian tradition. As Robert L. Calhoun explained:

> Anselm makes it possible for God to forgive without loss of perfect righteousness. The law has been fulfilled now. The penalty has been

paid, not in the form of punishment, but in the form of satisfaction, according to the principle: either punishment or satisfaction. Either will suffice. God's righteousness has been vindicated, and his mercy has been made immediately applicable to those men upon whom it is his good pleasure to have mercy.[14]

Anselm knew that forgiveness is not simple. Forgiveness does not say that what one did or did not do does not matter. Forgiveness declares that the guilt has been borne and the new possibilities of life are now offered. Something like this always happens in human relationships when one person forgives another. Whenever there is true forgiveness, there is always, as H. R. Mackintosh puts it, the suffering of atonement, which accepts the wrongdoing and bears the guilt on the part of the forgiver, and the suffering of repentance on the part of those who receive forgiveness.[15] The death of Jesus Christ belongs to the very being of God, and to receive God's forgiveness calls forth the suffering of repentance.

From the beginning, the Christian community always insisted that God's salvation has to be appropriate to the world which God has made. God cannot simply by fiat declare human beings saved. He cannot forgive out of a general disposition. Salvation has to come in ways that are appropriate in the light of the nature of God, the moral structure of the universe, and the nature of human existence itself. Anselm's way of understanding the forgiveness of God is the most profound in the history of the Christian community because it attempts to say that salvation is appropriate. It is the answer to the question of whether history, both public and individual, is simply a series of judgments, or whether there are resources of divine mercy which can overcome sin and evil without sacrificing the divine intention for human life. For Anselm and for Calvin, the heart of salvation is to be found in the death of Jesus Christ. The good news is paradoxically the death of Christ, a death which bought our salvation. The death of Christ could have been seen as the fate of a good life in a world dominated by evil persons. It could have been seen as an example of the way in which we are to respond to evil. The early Christian community, however, saw it neither as a terrible fate nor as a godly example, but as the redemptive act of God. The death of Christ is the actualization in human history of what happens in the very being of God. God takes our sin upon himself and forgives us. The atonement is the answer to George Bernard Shaw's contention that "forgiveness is a beggar's refuge; we must pay our debts."[16] The debt or the penalty or the satisfaction has been paid. This understanding of our salvation is the most profound of all.

It is worth noting that from the beginning Christians have recognized that the death of Christ belonged to the very being of God. When they spoke of God as impassible (without suffering) they meant, as G. L. Prestige has argued, that God was not swayed from without, in the way that human beings are at the mercy of those they love, but that God's activity in providence, redemption, and sanctification comes from the will of God. His love is not wrung from him by pity. This means that God is the same yesterday, today, forever. In this sense the death of Christ belongs in the very being of God. In the incarnation of the Son of God, God took death into his own being.

Yet the Christian community has never allowed what Anselm had to say to stand alone. Very quickly, within a century, Abailard (1079–1142) caricatured what Anselm had been saying by contending that it would be cruel and wicked to demand the blood of an innocent person as the price for anything, or that God should consider the death of his Son so agreeable that by it he should be reconciled to the whole world. For Abailard, the work of Christ was not the bearing of our sins so much as it was the manifestation of the outgoing love of God, which lays hold of us and frees us from slavery to sin and wins us for the true liberty of sons of God so that we do all things out of love rather than fear.[17]

Anselm is surely more profound, and without Anselm's understanding of the cost of forgiveness, no doctrine of the atonement is satisfactory. It can also be said that without Abailard's emphasis upon the whole work of Christ as the outreaching love of God, no other understanding is complete either.

God's great work for our redemption in Jesus Christ cannot be adequately stated or summarized in neatly written sentences or propositions. Salvation is God's confronting us in a person. On the purely human level no personal engagement can be exhaustively described in words. Yet various facets of what God did to redeem us are clear enough. Our salvation is the work of God in Christ, who did for us what we could not do for ourselves. He suffered vicariously for us, made satisfaction for our sins, and in the person of Jesus not only condemned sin but overcame sin and death. Yet God's salvation is also the outreaching of the love of God and the demonstration of God's will for human beings in Jesus Christ which elicits and evokes love and discipleship in us. This is the truth in the old evangelical way of describing salvation as coming to know Jesus. Jesus came preaching the kingdom of God and calling people to repentance. More than that, he was in his own life the embodiment of that kingdom in human history. As the risen Lord, he is the

Lord of the church in which we prepare for the coming of the kingdom in glory.

The Resurrection of Jesus Christ

The gospel is the death of Jesus Christ. The gospel is also the resurrection of Jesus Christ from the dead.

The resurrection of Jesus Christ is not simply a historical event, though the New Testament never understands it to be less than that. Just as the death of Christ must always be seen as more than a historical event, so the resurrection must be seen as at least a historical event, or so it is portrayed in the New Testament.

The New Testament consistently speaks of the resurrection as something that happened in time and space, that is concrete and objective. But it always speaks of the resurrection as something overpowering, something of a puzzlement, something of a mystery. The New Testament never envisaged Jesus Christ entering history again. The first Christians believed that God by a mighty act had raised Jesus Christ from the dead, empowering him to represent the kingdom of God in history. The disciples were witnesses to that elevation because God had made Jesus Christ visible to them. The power and unanimity of the New Testament witness is impressive.

Karl Barth, while recognizing the unique character of the resurrection, has emphasized the reality of the resurrection as an event that happened in time and space.

> If Jesus Christ is not risen—bodily, visibly, audibly, perceptibly, in the same concrete sense in which he died, as the texts themselves have it—if he is not also risen, then our preaching and our faith are vain and futile; we are still in our sins. And the apostles are found "false witnesses" because they have "testified of God that he raised up Jesus Christ, whom he raised not up" (1 Cor. 15:14f.). If they were true witnesses of his resurrection, they were witnesses of an event which was like that of the cross in its concrete objectivity. . . . The apostles witnessed that Jesus Christ risen from the dead had encountered them, not in the way in which we might say this (metaphorically) of a supposed or actual immanence of the existence, presence and action of the transcendent God, not in an abstract but in a concrete otherness, in the mystery and glory of the Son of God in the flesh. . . . We can therefore say quite calmly—for this is the truth of the matter—that they attested the fact that he made known to them this side of his (and their) death wholly in the light of the other side, and therefore that he made known to them the other side, his (and their) life beyond, wholly in terms of

this side, even as spoken in his resurrection from the dead, as the Yes of God to him (and therefore to them and to all men) concealed first under the No of his (and their) death.[18]

Barth likewise emphasizes the role of the empty tomb as a guide to understanding the resurrection.

> It is, in fact, an indispensable accompaniment of the attestation. It safeguards its content from misunderstanding in terms of a being of the Resurrected which is purely beyond or inward. It distinguishes the confession that Jesus Christ lives from a mere manner of speaking on the part of believers. It is the negative presupposition.of the concrete objectivity of his being. Let those who would reject it be careful—as in the case of the Virgin Birth—that they do not fall into Docetism.[19]

The New Testament is simple and chaste in what it declares. There is very little of the baroque and sensational that characterizes the apocryphal accounts. No one witnessed the resurrection. The New Testament simply declares, "This Jesus God raised up, and of that we all are witnesses" (Acts 2:32). The New Testament writers assume that Jesus was raised in a way congruent with the empty tomb. While they do not expect Jesus to enter again into their history, they do not doubt that he was raised up, that he is alive, that he was seen by them, and that he spoke to them. Any interpretation of the resurrection as a vision, hallucination, an event in the human heart contradicts the New Testament witness. Moreover, it leaves one to the mercy of the impersonal powers that seem relentlessly to govern this world, leading not only to our deaths as individuals but to the extinction of life on this planet. The resurrection means that the ultimate power is not the impersonal forces but the purposive loving action of God. The possibility of the resurrection rests upon the power of God to act personally in the created order. The question of the resurrection is finally a question about God and God's action in the world.

We cannot reconstruct what happened in the resurrection of Jesus Christ and in his appearances to his disciples. Karl Barth emphasized that the resurrection was not historical in the sense that it could be obverved independently of the standpoint of the onlooker.[20] It is not historical in the sense that it is analogous with other events in history. The death of Jesus can be described as simply an event in history, but not the resurrection. The New Testament did not speak of the resurrection as the revivification of a dead body or as a return to earthly life. The resurrection is the transformation of the body of Jesus into a reality unknown to us. Paul spoke of the change from a physical, perishable, and mortal body to a spiritual body (1 Cor. 15). We may speculate that the energy of the physical body was translated in the energy of the resurrected body in such a manner that his disciples recognized him. It was Jesus of Nazareth who was raised from the dead, and the disciples who had known him in the flesh recognized him as the crucified Christ. As such the resurrection is a mighty act of God, not the consequence of physical and historical causes. It is historical in that the disciples were witnesses and the validity of their witness was confirmed by their lives.

The resurrection is the mighty act of God which overturned what wicked people had done, which conquered death, which vindicated the life of Jesus, which made the risen Jesus present to his disciples, and which empowered him to represent the kingdom of God in history. Yet the resurrection is more than this. In Jesus' appearances to the disciples, the disciples were established in their discipleship, commissioned and sent forth into all the world to baptize, to teach, and to make disciples of all people.

The resurrection of Jesus Christ is gospel because it is an event that happened in time and space, because the risen Christ was seen, heard, and known by his disciples. The importance of this clear affirmation of the New Testament is made vivid in Rodion Shchedrin's oratorio, *Lenin in the People's Heart,* where the red guardsman sings at Lenin's deathbed, "No, no, no, no, that cannot be. Lenin lives, lives Lenin!"[21] Lenin lives in the cause, in memory, in the heart. This means there will come a time when cause, memory, and heart also die. Paul put the issue very clearly: "If Christ has not been raised, then our preaching is in vain and your faith is in vain. . . . But in fact Christ has been raised from the dead" (1 Cor. 15:14, 20).

The resurrection is good news for at least four reasons.

First, the resurrection was a divine confirmation of the life of Jesus Christ, of his words and of his deeds. As Barth puts it, it was the verdict of the Father. It declares that what Jesus Christ said and did is undergirded by the power of him who created the world and in whose power the world exists. Indeed, Paul speaks of God as the One who calls that which was not into being and who raises the dead (Rom. 4:17).

The resurrection, second, is the gospel because it is an answer to the problem of historical evil. In the past, human beings have been acutely aware of physical evil. In the eighteenth century, the Lisbon earthquake, for example, called in question Christian faith. In the twentieth century, the foundations of Christian faith have been called in question for many persons by radical, historical evil. The Jewish holocaust raises the problem not only of the chosen people but of God. How can we believe in God in a world where good people are so much at the mercy of evil people and of the events of history?

On Good Friday a good man named Jesus was put to death by a

weak and vacillating Roman governor named Pilate, a conniving high priest, Caiaphas, and howling, senseless demonstrators. On Good Friday evening it appeared as though the Pilates, the Caiaphases, and the demonstrators of this world represent reality. On Good Friday one could only wish that the world had such a structure that it supported the life of a good person such as Jesus. And therefore the disciples were in despair. They went back to the "real" world, to their fishing boats. But God raised Jesus Christ from the dead on Easter morning, undoing what wicked and evil persons had done on Good Friday.

superceding

Martin Niemöller published a very significant sermon in the midst of the German church struggle with the title, "But God."[22] He pointed out that on Good Friday the forces of evil seemed triumphant. But God raised Jesus Christ from the dead and undid what they had done. Therefore the Hitlers of this world, the Pilates, the Caiaphases, and the demonstrators in the streets have to barricade themselves against the word that is spoken beyond the grave, the resurrection of Jesus Christ.

The resurrection is, third, an answer to the problem of physical evil. Paul Tillich has said that the *Crucifixion* of Matthias Grünewald (c. 1470–1528) is the greatest portrayal of the incarnation in visual art.[23] The basis for this judgment is the sheer horror of the dead body upon the cross and the obvious anguish of those who stood at the foot of the cross. It puts in visual form the theological question of the incarnation: Can this man be the Son of God? Physical evil is devastating in dramatic forms like tornadoes and earthquakes, and in forms that more frequently affect us individually, such as cancer. On Good Friday physical evil had devastated a beautiful, wonderful life. Is this the way it ends? But God raised Jesus Christ from the dead, demonstrating in human history that there are resources of divine mercy and power that can take the broken, wounded pieces of life and put them together again.

The resurrection is a gospel for still a fourth reason. The risen Christ lives and sends forth his Spirit. The Spirit of Christ is the presence of the risen Christ in the world and the power of the risen Christ to work out his purposes in individual lives and in human communities. The power and presence of the Spirit of the risen Christ in the life of the church has confirmed the witness to the resurrection.

The resurrection means that human beings can be forgiven and also that they can be transformed. The New Testament speaks with enthusiasm about those who are in Christ being a new creation. Those who quake in the presence of life's perils can learn to live with serenity. Those who have been self-centered and brutal can become humane, open to their neighbor and ready to forgive. Those who have lived without purpose can understand their routine lives to be at least a broken fulfillment of the purposes of the Creator. Those who have lived irresponsibly can come to know they are obligated and answerable to God. This transformation happened in the New Testament, and it happens today by the power of the Spirit of the risen Christ.

The forgiveness of sins is the presupposition of the Christian life, not its goal. The forgiveness of sins is for the purpose of sanctification, the transformation of human life into the image of God. The forgiveness of sins is also the presupposition of the consummation of all things, when every knee shall bow and every tongue shall confess that Jesus Christ is Lord of all. The gospel is the power of God unto salvation which on the one hand forgives our sins and on the other restores in us the divine image. It is the gospel of the death of Jesus Christ for our sins and of his resurrection for our salvation.

4

God's Providing, Ordering, and Caring

The Christian witness is that the last word in every human situation is the grace of God. God's grace is not only forgiveness and renewal but also, as Reinhold Niebuhr says, God's "providential working in history by which he makes the wrath of man to praise him and transmutes good out of evil." The Lord had said to Paul, "My grace is sufficient for you, for my power is made perfect in weakness" (2 Cor. 12:9). The human situation may become difficult, but there is always hope. "We are afflicted in every way, but not crushed; perplexed, but not driven to despair; persecuted, but not forsaken; struck down, but not destroyed" (2 Cor. 4:8–9). Paul's clearest declaration of the grace of God in the midst of human perplexity comes in the triumphant close of his discussion of God's salvation in the letter to the Romans. "We know that in everything God works for good with those who love him" (Rom. 8:28). He concludes with the assurance, "In all these things we are more than conquerors through him who loved us. For I am sure that neither death, nor life, . . . nor anything else in all creation, will be able to separate us from the love of God in Christ Jesus our Lord" (Rom. 8:37–39).

The Grace of God's Providence

These affirmations of the grace of God in every human situation are a consequence of having experienced the presence of God in Jesus Christ.

This confidence that God's grace can be experienced in the ordinary affairs of life, the Creator's providing, ordering, and caring for his creation and, in particular, for human beings, is concretely expressed in the words of Jesus. In the heart of the Sermon on the Mount there occur the very remarkable words that relate God's care to the order of nature.

Therefore I tell you, do not be anxious about your life, what you shall eat or what you shall drink, nor about your body, what you shall put on. Is not life more than food, and the body more than clothing? Look at the birds of the air: they neither sow nor reap nor gather into barns, and yet your heavenly Father feeds them. Are you not of more value than they? . . . And why are you anxious about clothing? Consider the lilies of the field, how they grow; they neither toil nor spin; yet I tell you, even Solomon in all his glory was not arrayed like one of these. But if God so clothes the grass of the field, which today is alive and tomorrow is thrown into the oven, will he not much more clothe you, O men of little faith? Therefore do not be anxious, saying, 'What shall we eat?' or 'What shall we drink?' or 'What shall we wear?' For the Gentiles seek all these things; and your heavenly Father know that you need them all.

(Matthew 6:25–26, 28–32)

These words of Jesus have been neglected in contemporary theology. They have had, as it were, a bad press. Liberalism used them with a naïveté about the goodness of the world that has prejudiced readers who have experienced the crises and the calamities of the past fifty to seventy-five years. The Barthians had a built-in prejudice against such piety as a source of natural theology. More recently, social activists have sometimes repudiated these words as encouraging passivity in the presence of injustice.

These biases against the clear piety of the passage do not reach the substance. It is not likely that those who first heard these words were naive either about the facts of human history or about the facts of nature. They were exposed to both nature and history without the many protections we now have. The impact of the presence of God in Jesus Christ was so great that they had no need for natural theology. Certainly they did not use the sayings as an excuse not to give a cup of cold water to the thirsty or bread to the hungry.

These words express a faith which sees in nature the grace of the Creator, a grace that was first experienced in Jesus Christ. The faith that God cares for his people in the order of nature as well as history is a faith which Jesus confers. His words declare with a directness that speaks to the human heart even in a scientific age that God the Creator of the universe is the Father who cares, not only for his creation but in particular for his people. They declare in language that is simple and unambiguous that even the most mundane structures of nature as well as history are open to the grace of God. God cares, and therefore we can trust him.

John Calvin insisted in a very remarkable passage that our first response to creation is not to understand it but to appreciate it as God's creation.[1] Indeed, he goes on to say that the attempt to understand nature—its structures, its causes, and its interrelationships—

may work against understanding nature as the creation of the God whom we know in Jesus Christ.

Faith in providence is simply another aspect of the awareness that God is personal, an awareness which lies at the root of most religious history. Christian confidence about the personal activity of God in nature and history, at least in the New Testament, is rooted in the experience of God's presence in the saving work of Jesus Christ, not in reflection either upon human experience or upon our experience of nature itself. Knowing God in Christ, we come to affirm that this world is God's world and that history and nature are open to God's gracious activity. After expounding what God in his righteousness has done for our salvation, Paul exclaims, "We know that in everything God works for good with those who love him" (Rom. 8:28).

The Christian witness to the world today is that God's grace is the last word in every human situation, whether that situation is a historical event that overwhelms us or a natural event that threatens us with destruction. This grace is not a human disposition that enables us with stoic discipline to face whatever happens. It is, rather, the personal gracious activity of God, which opens up new possibilities and gives hope beyond every defeat.

A personal disposition would enable us to face life's challenges with dignity but not with hope. God's grace does not give us simply an attitude, but a hope that enables us to use creatively whatever comes toward the final fulfillment of God's purposes for us and for his creation. An old hymn that has been frequently sung of late expresses this faith in memorable words:

> Through many dangers, toils, and snares
>   I have already come;
> 'Tis grace has brought me safe thus far,
>   And grace will lead me home.

The grace which is the last word is not a psychological nostrum that enables us to endure but the powerful gracious presence of God, who will lead us home.

Augustine, at the beginning of the *City of God,* had to face the question, Why did Christians suffer the same brutality and the same violence as non-Christians?[2] He had to deal with the particularly violent crime of rape. Augustine explains that if the barbarians had not been introduced to Christianity, the plight of Christian and non-Christian alike would have been worse. Then he proceeds to give the real answer. Christians are distinguished not by what happens to them but by the way they respond to what happens to them. "For even in the likeness of the sufferings, there remains an unlikeness in the sufferers; and though exposed to the same anguish, virtue and vice are not the same thing. The great difference between human beings is found not in what ills they suffer, but in what kind of persons suffer them." Christians differ from other people, not in what happens to them, but in the fact that they respond in faith, hope, and love.

The Christian witness is that there is a grace, the living, active personal presence of God, available in all historical events and in all natural events, particularly as natural events impinge on human lives. This grace is the final word in every such event, and through this grace a person is enabled not only to determine the significance of what happens to him or her, but also to use everything in history and nature in the achieving of the purposes of God. This means there are no dead-end streets in life in which evil is the last word, no enclosures from which there is no exit.

God and the World

The rise of modern science and history as autonomous disciplines has made it increasingly difficult for Christian people to experience in nature or even in history itself the presence and in particular the gracious presence of God. Scientific textbooks describe nature in terms of laws that operate according to their own energies and principles. These scientific studies appear to explain nature without leaving any room for God's activity. Knowing how the world works is so impressive that the more fundamental question of why the world works at all is obscured. Moreover, the explanations appear so complete and without remainder there seems to be no place for God's gracious activity. The scientific and naturalistic ethos of our time tempts us to reduce God's activity to God's address, to the fact that God speaks to us through the events of nature. Whether finally it is easier or more credible to believe that God speaks through the events of nature and history or to trust that God actively and personally participates in those events is not clear. Over and over again in the history of theology the attempts to make faith in God more relevant or more congruent with contemporary culture have turned out to require the same leap of faith as the articles they replaced.

In any case, the Bible from beginning to end affirms the personal activity of God in both nature and history. And this witness is so clear that it makes doubtful that any form of Christian faith is viable which does not include an affirmation of the living God who works personally in the created order. Herbert Butterfield remarked: "Of all the factors which have operated to the disadvantage of religion and the undermining of religious sense in recent centuries, the most damaging has been the notion of an absentee God who might be supposed to have created the universe in the first place, but who is assumed to have left it to run as a piece of clockwork, so that he is outside our lives, outside of history."[3] This is a theological judgment, but it is a theological judgment that is confirmed by the commonsense wisdom of the church as the people of God or, to put it more theologically, confirmed by the testimony of the Holy Spirit in the life of the church. Theologies that minimize the living God and the personal activity of God in the created order may survive in academic communities; however, their survival power in the history of Christian communities, and in particular in the worshiping, believing community of faith, is very limited.

The scriptures everywhere assume the immediacy of God's activity in his creation. John Calvin in the sixteenth century could say vigorously and firmly that not a wind blows and not a drop of rain falls without the express command of God.[4] Here we have the kind of immediacy in God's relationship to the world that the psalmist expressed:

> May the glory of the LORD endure for ever,
> may the LORD rejoice in his works,
> who looks on the earth and it trembles,
> who touches the mountains and they smoke!
> I will sing to the LORD as long as I live;
> I will sing praise to my God while I have being.
> (Psalm 104:31–33)

The question we have to face is whether this sense of the immediacy of the activity of God, which is expressed in every page of the Old Testament and also in every page that Calvin ever wrote, is possible for those who live in a post-Enlightenment, post-scientific-revolution world.

A basic problem for Christian piety today is the recovery of an awareness of this world as God's creation in which we know his presence. Any such recovery that is enduring must go beyond the emotional and the aesthetic. It must include rational reflection on how God works in his creation and on the various forces that play their roles in all the events in which we participate and which happen to us. Any such reflection must relate human life first of all to what seems to be the stable order of the universe; second, to human freedom; and third, to the possible openness of nature and history to the personal action of God.

How can we relate these convictions to the world we know?

First, we can accept God's ordering of the universe, his provision of the structures, the natures, and the processes and energy systems as God's gracious gift.[5] The world has structures, processes, and na-

tures, as well as energy systems, which can be analyzed in the labora-
tory and described with some precision in scientific textbooks. Scientific study has enabled us to harness these powers for human good.
We can fly in the airplane, overcoming many of the problems of
space, and we can devise medicines that protect us against many
diseases. The scientific description of the universe is very impressive,
not simply in what it has contributed to our comfort and convenience
but also in the completeness of the explanation. We have confidence
that all secrets will be open to investigation and disclosure. In actual
fact, the universe is not as open to our investigations as it first appears, and on further examination, the secrets of how the universe
operates seem very resistant to our mastery of them by human intelligence. Yet our knowledge of how the world works is sufficiently
impressive that it has obscured the more fundamental question of
why there is a world anyway and why it works at all.

Yet the question remains: Can we, in the piety of the church,
come to see that the reliability of the world's structures is an expression of the divine purpose? When G. K. Chesterton declared
that the sun rose every morning because God said, "Get up!" or
when George Buttrick declared that the regularity of nature is but
the faithfulness of God, their statements contradict the seemingly
independent structures and processes of nature which we experience.[6] Can we sing and mean that God has brought us safely
through another day or week? Can we praise God every morning
for the rising of the sun, seeing in it evidence of a providence operative not only in his creation but also in his continuing care and
ever-present activity?

One of the most influential poems in our tradition, and also a
confession of Christian faith, which we still sing, is Francis of Assisi's
"Canticle of the Sun."

> All creatures of our God and King,
> Lift up your voice and with us sing. . . .
>
> Thou flowing water, pure and clear,
> Make music for thy Lord to hear. . .
>
> And all ye men of tender heart,
> Forgiving others, take your part.
> Ye who long pain and sorrow bear,
> Praise God and on him cast your care!

The hymn omits Francis's final exclamation of faith when he ad-
dresses death as "our sister the death of the body."[7] Francis was
certain that this world is God's creation. He accepted what we call
the laws of nature as God's gracious gift.

The acceptance of the impartial, law-abiding structure of nature as the proper context for the Christian life is at the basis of Christian piety. The Christian life is not a search for special favors from God, but the acceptance of the law-abiding quality of the world as one of the means by which God brings us to human maturity. The crucial question is whether the law-abiding quality of the world is regarded as our fate or as God's gracious gift. This is finally a matter of faith, not of science, depending more on the community of worship and theological discourse in which we live and not so much on the latest scientific textbook we have read.

Such a faith is not simple today or in any day. Modern science has made God unnecessary for many people, reliably providing us with things for which people in the past prayed with uncertain results. Moreover, the psychological impressiveness of the stability and predictability of nature as well as the textbooks of science make it incredible for some that nature is the expression of intentionality and purpose and not simply of impersonal forces. The challenge to faith and the task of theology is to recover an awareness that nature is the intention and order of a gracious God without denying the truths about nature's reliability and predictability which science has discovered and which greatly enhance our physical comfort and health.

The second step toward acceptance of human freedom as God's gracious gift is an increased awareness that this is the world that God made. One of the most mysterious facts in the history of the universe is the emergence of the human self with the power of the human spirit. The human self has the capacity to objectify its own existence, to pass judgment upon that existence, and to organize all the energies and vitalities of this life in pursuit of a goal chosen in the light of that evaluation.

Human beings are creatures of instinct and of impulse just as animals are, but human beings know that they are. They can objectify and reflect upon the instincts and impulses that impinge upon their personal existence. This gives a certain freedom over instinct and impulse. When food is placed in the presence of a hungry dog, the dog eats. When food is placed in the presence of a hungry human being, he or she may or may not eat. A human person is free not to eat—in order to lose weight, for example, or in order to feed hungry people in a distant portion of the world, whom one has not seen and whose need one knows only in the imagination. This capacity of the human self to stand outside the self and to objectify the self's existence gives us a freedom not only over nature, but also over history and over our own personal past.

This human freedom complicates every human act which in the animal would be only a natural act, and also every event in the natural world. We read in the newspapers about devastating floods, about the consequences of volcanic eruptions, about drought, but we do not always remember that floods, volcanic eruptions, and droughts are always complicated by human freedom. In our freedom we create the conditions in which these natural events are far more devastating, or in our freedom we can create situations that modify the devastations of floods, of droughts, and of volcanic eruptions.

The role of human freedom in our own personal interaction with nature as well as with history is clear enough. In most events in our lives, there is an interaction of the nature which we can describe in scientific textbooks, of the history of human communities, and of our own human response to nature and to human history. When we relate the events of history and of our own personal lives to human freedom, new possibilities are opened for us to see the grace and the mercy of God at work in our lives.

The third step toward relating our convictions to the world we know is to recognize that while God made the world, with structures, natures, orders, and energy systems that can be scientifically described, and while he gave to human beings freedom in their interaction with this world, he also created the world so that nature and history are open to reason, love, and grace. This is true on the human level. Human reason, love, and grace can interact with nature and history even in the most complicated and most overwhelming situations to modify those situations.

This leads us a step further to the really crucial affirmation, which is that God has created the world, if the scriptural witness is true, so that the so-called order of nature and the structures of human history are open to the purposive action of God. This affirmation does not require divine intervention in the natural order or the historical order in ways which set aside the structures, natures, and energy systems that govern the world of nature and history, or the abuse of human freedom. It is to say that God has made the world so that it is responsive to his purposive intentions without any such intervention. Nathaniel Micklem once used the analogy of a human blush as an indication of how the world of nature is open to God's intentional activity.[8] A blush is a very human act. It arises out of the embarrassment of the self, which is expressed in the flushed coloring of the human face. The self does not intervene in the natural processes that govern the human body, but the human body is open to the intentionality and the purposes of the self. In some such way, the world in which we live is open to the grace of God.

This means that the world of nature and history is open to the purposive action of God, and it means that petitionary prayer is not vain babbling. Karl Barth has pointed out that petition is the very essence of prayer.

> Nor can we reject too strongly those theories which seek to restrict the significance of prayer to the subjective sphere alone. If this presupposition can be made, then whenever the Christian believes and obeys and prays there does not merely take place a creaturely movement. But concealed within the creaturely movement, yet none the less really, there moves the finger and hand and sceptre of the God who rules the world. And what is more, there moves the heart of God, and he himself is there in all the fulness of his love and wisdom and power.[9]

Ian Barbour, a physicist-theologian, has suggested that a person's answer to the question, Is it proper theologically to pray for rain? reveals that person's real theology.[10] Does God personally act in the created order? The answer to this question depends upon our doctrine of God and how we conceptualize God's relation to the world.

The Bible emphasizes the immediacy of God's control of the world. The Old Testament thinks of God's relationship to the world very much as a king to his dominion. John Calvin declared that not a wind blows and not a raindrop falls without the express command of God.[11] The stability of the order which modern science has found in the world makes it difficult to think in this way of God's relation to the world.

Newtonian science and the theologians who were associated with Newton popularized the image of God as that of a clockmaker.[12] Great clocks, such as a famous one at Strasbourg, when once built needed only occasional attention from the clockmaker. The clockmaker was in his space and the clock in its space. When necessary, the clockmaker could come to the assistance of the clock. This became a model of God's relation to the world, especially in popular piety. On occasion God did fix the world (his clock) or "pass a miracle." Miracles became "intervention" in the natural order and thus unintelligible to many persons who had studied science or who had learned to live without God.

Some found a way out of the difficulty of conceiving of God's action in a scientific world by limiting God's activity to history or, more particularly, to God's address or speech. Yet history and nature are too closely related for the limitation of the action of God in history to be satisfactory. Nature, as at Dunkirk, mightily shapes history. The limitation of God's action to God's address stands in sharp contradiction to the Bible and to the critical judgment of popular piety. On the level of congregational piety, a theology which asserts that God speaks through the natural order but does not purposefully act in it is not persuasive. If the traditional way of thinking about God's relationship to the world is too immediate, it is also true that the image of the clockmaker or the God who speaks but does not influence nature or history is not plausible. Human lives are too much involved in history and in nature to affirm speech without action.

God's relation to the world can be conceptualized, as has been noted, according to an analogy of the self and the body. This analogy also may be too immediate to do justice to the structure God has given the world. Yet it points in the right direction. God's relationship to the world, his transcendence and immanence, can best be understood in personal terms, according to the way a person is transcendent to and yet immanent in his action.

No modern theology has so clearly understood God's transcendence and immanence in personal categories as that of William Temple.

> A person is properly described as transcendent of his acts. He is expressed in these, but he has an existence apart from them. . . . *What a true doctrine of divine transcendence will assert is not a reservoir of normally unutilised energy, but a volitional as contrasted with a mechanical direction of the energy utilised.* [13]

William Temple may emphasize the personal activity of God in the natural order beyond what many find to be true, as in the following paragraph:

> If we adopt this view, we shall have also to hold that no Law of Nature as discovered by physical science is ultimate. It is a general statement of that course of conduct in Nature which is sustained by the purposive action of God so long and so far as it will serve His purpose. No doubt it is true that the same cause will always produce the same effect in the same circumstances. Our contention is that an element in every actual cause, and indeed the determinant element, is the active purpose of God fulfilling itself with that perfect constancy which calls for an infinite graduation of adjustments in the process. Where any adjustment is so considerable as to attract notice it is called a miracle; but it is not a specimen of a special class, it is an illustration of the general character of the World-Process.[14]

Temple may not do justice to the independence of the natural order, just as Calvin did not until his emphasis upon the immediacy of God's control was called in question by the pantheistic libertines. Nevertheless, Temple's discussion of this theological problem offers more hope of an intelligible understanding of God's relationship to the world that does justice to the independence of the natural order, and that leaves nature and history open to God's purposive action, than any other conceptuality seems to do.

Reflection on life in the world, asking what God was saying through the joys and disappointments, the successes and the defeats, through unexpected events that enhance our lives as well as accidents or illness that thwart our purpose, was part of Christian piety until recently. It was certainly fundamental for John Calvin. The increasing isolation of nature and history from God has undermined faith and piety, at least the piety of which Jesus spoke in the Sermon on the Mount. Furthermore, the practical fact that science does for us what we used to ask of God gives us the illusion we can live with no reference to providence. As Harry Emerson Fosdick pointed out in a great sermon, we used to pray for everything from babies to good crops.[15] Today we consult the doctor or the agronomist. Practical atheism may be more destructive of piety than theoretical atheism.

The recovery of this piety today must accept as God's gracious gift the stability and reliability of the natural order. It is this order which makes life, as we know it, possible. It must also reflect on the role of human freedom, not only in accidents but in such "natural" disasters as floods, famine, and tornadoes. Finally, Christian piety must without presumption be open to personal acts of God: that is, to events which are transparent to God's purposes at least for persons of faith who participate in them. The Christian life includes and can hardly be lived without this reflection on the ways in which God is present in the various events of life. How has God acted and what is God saying to me in varied events of my life?

The question of God's providence comes to a focus for many people in the problem of accidents. God has made the world so that it is precarious. Life cannot be lived without the risk of accident as well as the risk of human freedom. How is God involved in the accidents that come to every person? How can we relate accidents theologically to our lives?

William Temple, on the basis of his understanding of how God works in creation, has illustrated the practical consequences of his theology in the discussion of accidents. An accident may be illustrated this way: A man is walking down the street. A brick falls off a chimney and hits him on the head, with fatal consequences. The falling of the brick is determined by natural laws that govern the construction of chimneys and the power of cement to hold bricks in place. Perhaps also the wind was a factor. The man's action was determined by free decision to walk down the street to visit a friend or to make a purchase at a neighboring store. An accident occurs when human conduct determined by human decisions is contradicted by an event governed by natural laws. No special act of God is involved except insofar as God did not work a miracle to change the direction of the person's journey.

The stability of natural laws is essential to human life and planning. The general laws which govern the universe are not contrary to the love of God but are rather an expression of that love. They serve human good. On occasion, however, a person is hit on the head by a falling brick or schoolchildren in a bus are drowned by a sudden flood. It is quite clear that God has made the world so that accidents happen, that life is precarious even for the most cautious of human beings. Having thus defined an accident, Temple then goes on to indicate how a universe that is precarious for human beings can be compatible with the love of God.

But why, if he is Love, does he not intervene to save his children from the occasional evils resulting from the action of those fixed laws? Could he not either divert the chimney-pot or breathe into my subconscious mind a suggestion that would prevent my walking where it was about to fall? People seldom ask these questions with reference to accidents that might befall themselves; but they ask them when their friends are concerned; and they pray that their friends may be preserved from such accidents. Is this reasonable? If not, is it because God cannot, or because he will not, intervene? In any case, what becomes of omnipotent Love?

I would answer first that God certainly can intervene and (moreover) that, in my belief, he often does; this cannot be proved, and it would be unsound to base any general philosophic view upon this conviction. The experience of religious people is, however, decisive to anyone who accepts the religious hypothesis. People who take care to keep their devotional life fresh and vigorous find repeatedly that they are "guided" to act or speak in ways the value of which is only afterwards appreciated. To maintain spiritual contact with God produces, it would seem, a sensitiveness to the Divine Will which usually shows itself only in the actions which it prompts. Personally I believe that a similar result may be produced by intercession.

When, therefore, some precious life is cut off by an accident, or when widespread devastation is caused, we should not say "Why does God choose to do this?" God does not "choose to do this"; what God chooses is to create a world to which "this" is incidental. And it is good for us all that he does. But while he does not specifically choose that the accident should occur, he is ready to support both those who die and those who remain on earth with the experience of his loving presence: He does not leave them merely in the grip of a mechanical universe grinding out its causal sequences, but by means of all that comes gives his children a new motive to find himself. Of course this argument is peculiarly irritating to the atheist or agnostic. The Christian finds confirmation of his faith whatever happens. If he has earthly happiness, he turns to God with thanksgiving; if he has earthly sorrow, he turns with renewed eagerness to the Eternal Love, and gives thanks for what impelled him thither once more. In all things that happen he finds God, not because he traces the eternal purpose in an infinite number of "particular providences," but because he has learnt how to make all temporal experience direct his attention to its eternal background. Consequently he "gives thanks at all times for all things," because he has found it literally true that "all things work together for good to them that love God."[16]

This openness of God's creation to the purpose and the grace of God is the basis for Christian experience in every generation. In all times and places, Christian people have been able to look back over their lives and render the testimony that, in the strange events of their own existence, they see the hand and the purpose of God. Moreover, in every time and in every place, Christian people have experienced certain events as uniquely expressive of God's purpose.

Christian piety accepts the order which God has given the world as the context for the Christian life. The piety of the Gospel and the teachings of the epistles exclude any notion that Christians should expect favors from God's providence. God causes his sun to rise on the evil and good alike and sends his rains equally on the just and the unjust (Matt. 5:45). There is a divine impartiality in the providence of God. William James once said that religion for many people was lobbying in the courts of the Almighty for special favors.[17] The New Testament teaches us that that piety is accepting the impartiality of nature as God's gracious gift and responding to it with faith, hope, and love. Christian piety is certainly not resignation, and it is more than consenting to the powers that impinge upon our lives. It is coming to accept the natural order, which can be so destructive of human hopes, as somehow the gracious activity of the God and Father of our Lord Jesus Christ. It is also living with the awareness that nature and history are open to the purposive action of God, which we cannot coerce or predict and which we must not presume.

God and Human History

Our understanding of God's grace in the governance of the world must be related to God's intention for human life. In the familiar words of the Shorter Catechism, the purpose of human life is to glorify God.[18] On the other hand, God's purpose on the human level is, in the words of Hebrews, to bring many sons to glory (Heb. 2:10) or, in the words of Paul, to nurture human beings into Christian maturity (Eph. 4:13; Col. 1:28). The human environment in nature and history must be understood in terms of these purposes.

John Hick has pointed out that the purpose of God in creating the world as a place for human life is very different from the purpose of a human being in building a cage or a pen for a pet animal.[19] The purpose in an environment for an animal is to make the animal as comfortable as possible. God's purpose in the provision of an environment for human nature is not primarily to provide for human comfort but for the possibilities of growth to human maturity.

Adam was created a mature human being, according to Augustine's conceptualization of human origins. In Augustine's language, he was created mutably good by an immutably good God.[20] Adam's mutable goodness could have become a confirmed goodness if Adam had obeyed and had responded to the challenges of life with faith and obedience.

Adam's fall, according to Augustine, did not take God by surprise, and God had made provision for the redemption of Adam in Jesus Christ.[21] This redemption is so great and wonderful that some could exclaim, "O happy fault, that caused so wonderful a redemption."

Irenaeus had a very different conceptual understanding of Adam, whom he regarded as an infant. This infant had been placed in the world, with its challenges and crises. In response to these challenges, Adam, the child, could grow to become a mature human being.[22]

Whether one understands Adam in terms of Augustine's mature human being or in terms of Irenaeus's child, the natural and historical context of human life provides the occasion for growing to human maturity. Sons of God, or mature human beings, are by definition beyond the creative power of God. God cannot create a mature human being; he can only create a human being with the possibility of growth to maturity. Human maturity comes as one responds to the frustrations, the disappointments, the crises, and the challenges of human life. A universe designed for human comfort and security would have made human maturity an impossibility.

Hence the Puritans regarded human history as the vale of soul-making, or the school for character. This understanding of human life and of the proper matrix for human growth enables us to see even in pain and suffering the grace of God by which God seeks to bring many souls to glory. The person who trusts in God can find a way to use everything that happens for the achieving of God's purposes for human life. John Calvin wrote to Madame Coligny concerning sickness, "It seems that illnesses must serve as medicines for us, to purge us of attachment to the world and to cut off what is superfluous in us."[23]

Christians in the New Testament saw everything that happened to them and to their world in the light of God's providence. Each event was a promise, a blessing, or a judgment of God. They interpreted what happened to them as a word of God. They continually asked, What did God mean or intend when he gave me this blessing, or when he placed this problem or challenge before me, or when he afflicted me in this particular way? This does not mean that the New Testament Christians—or Calvin, who likewise believed in this providential care of God in the sixteenth century—had little regard for human actions and for second causes. The New Testament Christians and Calvin alike were aware of the importance of what human beings do and the relative independence of the natural order of things. But each saw God working in and through the order he established. Modern knowledge has changed the way we conceptualize the problem. We no longer think in the same categories as did the Christians of either the first century or the sixteenth century, but, as Herbert Butterfield has remarked, the different categories do not nullify the same reality which they faced then and which we face today. "For let us make sure of one thing—in the long run, there are only two alternative views about life or about history. Here is a fact which was realized thousands of years ago and it is still as true as ever. Either you trace everything back in the long run to sheer blind chance, or you trace everything to God."[24]

According to Butterfield, there are three ways of looking at any historical event.[25] The first he calls biographical, in which human beings take actions and make decisions operating with a certain measure of freedom. The Christian, Butterfield says, must be very emphatic that human freedom plays its role in the shaping of events. The second way of looking at history is historical, that is, a scientific examination of the deep forces and tendencies in history, tendencies that overwhelm individuals and their freedom. The historical way of seeing history makes us aware that the real tragedies in human history are not acts of sheer perversity but are in part the product of forces in history that develop, as it were, over the heads of human beings and help to produce a French revolution, or an industrial revolution, or a great war. There is a third aspect of history, according to Butterfield:

> Either you must say that Chance is one of the greatest factors in history, and that the whole of the story is in the last resort the product of blind chance, or you must say that the whole of it is in the hands of providence—in him we live and move and have our being—even the free will of men, and even the operation of law in history, even these are within providence itself, and under it.[26]

Yet providence must not be conceived in a capricious way. We must begin by seeing how God works in our individual lives, and then we expand on this on the scale of nature and project it on the scale of humankind. The way God reveals himself in history is in fact the great theme of the Bible itself. In the Bible, history is understood in terms of the promise punctuated by judgment, but always under the promise. Another and more theological way of putting this is to say that the Christian task is to see history not simply in terms of scientific law and not simply in terms of human freedom, and certainly not in terms of chance, but in terms of the working of God, who has made known his ways to us in Jesus Christ. The Christian learns to discern in the routine of life God's blessings and chastisements, God's testing and beckoning, God's judgment and redemption, and having learned to discern God's providence in personal life is equipped to behold the hand of God in history.

The Christian gospel that the church has to proclaim to our day is the grace of God, which is operative in nature and in history. No historical event and no force of nature as it impinges on a human life is ever simply reducible to human freedom or to the operation of the structures and laws and natures and energy systems with which God has endowed his creation. Human freedom and nature itself are open to the grace of God, which, it is our faith, works with those who love God to bring good out of every situation. It is this grace that enables ordinary people to live gracefully, with serenity and poise, amid the vicissitudes of their lives and in the presence of the final test of faith for us all: namely, death.

Two great hymns of our faith have stated this better than the theologians. They have served as confessions of faith and as the means by which the faith has been taught and learned. The first ("How Firm a Foundation") is a rendition of Isaiah 40–41:

> Fear not, I am with thee, O be not dismayed,
> For I am thy God, I will still give thee aid. . . .
>
> When through the deep waters I call thee to go,
> The rivers of sorrow shall not overflow.

The second ("If Thou But Suffer God to Guide Thee") is a paraphrase of Psalm 55:

> Who trusts in God's unchanging love
> Builds on the rock that nought can move. . . .
>
> God never yet forsook at need
> The soul that trusted him indeed.

5

Chosen Before the Foundation of the World

Human existence is a puzzlement. The emergence of the human mind and of the person in the history of the universe is a fact, but also a mystery. Jacques Monod, a Nobel laureate in biology, gave one answer to the mystery.

> Man must at last wake out of his millenary dream and discover his total solitude, his fundamental isolation. He must realize that, like a gypsy, he lives on the boundary of an alien world; a world that is deaf to his music, and as indifferent to his hopes as it is to his suffering or his crimes.
>
> Who, then, is to define crime? Who decides what is good and what is evil? All the traditional systems placed ethics and values beyond man's reach. Values did not belong to him; they were imposed on him, and he belonged to them. Today he knows that they are his and his alone, but now he is master of them they seem to be dissolving in the uncaring emptiness of the universe. It is at this point that modern man turns toward science, or rather against it, now seeing its terrible capacity to destroy not only bodies but the soul itself.[1]

Arthur Koestler, who carried on his polemic against communism in astutely written novels, has the question put to the communist in *Darkness at Noon:* Who is an individual? The communist replies, in substance: An individual is a multitude of a million divided by a million—a cipher.[2]

The Christian understanding of what it means to be a human being in the world was proclaimed by Paul in chaste, direct, plain words, as a fitting summary of what he understood God's salvation to mean:

> We know that in everything God works for good with those who love him, who are called according to his purpose. For those whom he foreknew he also predestined to be conformed to the image of his Son, in order that he might be the first-born among many brethren. And

those whom he predestined he also called; and those whom he called
he also justified; and those whom he justified he also glorified.
(Romans 8:28–30)

A similar passage in Ephesians 1:4–5 declares that God chose his
people before the foundation of the world. We celebrate this truth
when we baptize a child, calling the child's name, for God gives the
child life, identity, individuality, a name. To be chosen before the
foundation of the world means that God (1) thought of us before we
were, (2) elected us to be his people, (3) gave us a work to do, (4)
called us to be sanctified, and finally (5) called us to glory.

Given a Name

The assumption that human beings are valuable in and of themselves has been easily made in a culture that has its roots in the
Christian tradition. But this assumption has been repeatedly called
into question, not only by scientists, novelists, and philosophers but
also by the dramatic events in history of the past century. Events
such as Stalin's harvest of terror in the Ukraine, or Mao's liquidation
of dissidents in China, or the Jewish holocaust, or the tragedy of
Cambodia, or the slaughter of a minority people in Nigeria or
Uganda remind us that it is far from clear that human beings in and
of themselves are valuable. More people have died in the twentieth
century by actions of governments that have in one way or the other
dispassionately decreed their death than by war in which they died
in violence and anger.[3]

The rhetoric of our time, whether it comes from democratic or
communist nations, from developed or undeveloped nations, speaks
about the importance of the individual. Yet this rhetoric seldom
centers on the importance of the individual simply as an individual,
and it seldom attempts to indicate why human beings should be
treated with respect, or their lives regarded as precious in and of
themselves. T. S. Eliot, that astute critic of our culture, has put it
dramatically: "A thousand policemen directing the traffic" cannot
tell us why we are here or where we are going.[4]

Nicholas Berdyaev, the Russian philosopher who died an exile in
Paris, once declared that where there is no God there is no man.[5] By
this he meant that if you leave God out of the picture, the value of
a person is determined only by belonging to the right class, or the
right race, or the right nation, or the right economic group. The
value of a human being is always determined by the group to which
he or she belongs. A person simply as a person has no value, Berdyaev
said, unless his or her existence is referred to God.

The New Testament answer to the puzzlement about human existence is nowhere more clearly put than in the letter to the Ephesians. Here it is declared that

> the God and Father of our Lord Jesus Christ . . . has blessed us in Christ with every spiritual blessing in the heavenly places, even as he chose us in him before the foundation of the world, that we should be holy and blameless before him. He destined us in love to be his sons through Jesus Christ, according to the purpose of his will, to the praise of his glorious grace which he freely bestowed on us in the Beloved.
>
> (Ephesians 1:3–6)

The preciousness of human life is not determined by our personal work, or by the group to which we belong, but by the fact that God thought of us before we were, called us into being, gave to us our individuality, our name, a dignity that no one dare abuse. Another way of putting it is in the words of Psalm 139.

> O LORD, thou hast searched me and known me!
> Thou knowest when I sit down and when I rise up;
>   thou discernest my thoughts from afar.
> . . . .
> Thou dost beset me behind and before,
>   and layest thy hand upon me.
>
> (Psalm 139:1–2, 5)

In the Gospels, Jesus declares that even the hairs on our heads are numbered. Human worth and dignity are established by the origin of every human life in the intention of God, and by the fact that God looks at us and knows us by name.

In a world in which human life is frequently overwhelmed by the impersonal forces and the seeming absurdities of both nature and history, the New Testament dares to declare that the origin of human existence and, indeed, human salvation, is prior to the creation of the world itself. Every human life is rooted in the intention of God. God thought of us before we were and called us into being.

Predestined

The God who calls us into being also elects us to be his people. God's grace precedes our decision. God chooses us before we choose God. This is the well-known doctrine of predestination. The doctrine presupposes human sin, but even if we had not sinned, God's gracious calling would precede our decision. The Christian life is a gift before it is a human achievement.

The most significant experiences in life are beyond the power of the human will. The human will is a remarkable capacity. It can organize the energies and vitalities of life in pursuit of a freely chosen goal. Human beings are not at the mercy of impulse and instinct and momentary need as animals are, so far as we know. We have a will. We ought to use our wills more than we do. But there are depths in human life which are beyond the will.

We cannot forget ourselves by trying hard. The more we try to forget ourselves, the more we think about ourselves.

We are not grateful by trying hard. By discipline of will, we can write thank-you notes according to Emily Post. But gratitude is not a product of discipline.

We cannot be humble by trying hard. If a proud man should become humble by trying hard, he would be proud of his humility.

We cannot love by trying hard. To say we ought to love comes very near to being a contradiction, for there is a spontaneity about love that is beyond the power of the will.

Now the human predicament, according to Christian faith, is self-centeredness. People, who ought to be God-centered, are ego-centered, judging everything by the way it affects the ego—myself, my race, my family, my church, my country. There is no way for self-centered human beings to become God-centered by their own efforts. There is no way for those who love themselves to force themselves to love God. This is the basic human predicament.

T. S. Eliot's great play *Murder in the Cathedral* is a splendid illustration of this universal human predicament. Thomas Becket had served his king well as chancellor. So when the king wanted control of the church, he appointed Thomas Archbishop of Canterbury. But Thomas became a great archbishop, defending the independence of the church. The controversy that followed between king and archbishop ended with the archbishop's martyrdom. While Thomas awaits his execution, Eliot pictures the tempters coming to him.

The first reminds him of the good old days when he and the king were friends, and of the good times they had on the river Thames. But Thomas easily dismisses the tempter. Some sins are effectively cured simply by old age.

Other tempters come to offer the prospect of chancellor's power again or an alignment with barons against the king. But Thomas has expected these tempters, and he rejects their pleas.

The fourth tempter comes unexpectedly. First he offers the glories of martyrdom, of pilgrimages to the grave, of miracles that would be done there. And then there is the added pleasure of thinking of your enemies "in another place." But Thomas has thought of these things too, and he knows that history has a way of exposing martyrs and discarding them. Now the tempter comes with the final thrust. No earthly glory can compare with heavenly grandeur. There is the final temptation to be last on earth in order to be first in heaven.

In agony, Thomas faces the tragedy of the "righteous." Sinful pride on one level of life is cast out only by more sinful pride on a higher level of "righteousness." This is the ultimate predicament and the ultimate temptation: "The last temptation is the greatest treason: / To do the right deed for the wrong reason."[6]

This is the predicament for which predestination is the answer. Lost human beings cease being self-centered, and the saints cease making themselves lowest on earth in order to be first in heaven, only when something happens to them which draws their attention from themselves, which moves the center of life from self to God.

It is our faith that this is what God has done through the life, death, and resurrection of Jesus Christ. God was in Christ reconciling the world to himself and doing for us what we could not do for ourselves.

The question *now* arises, How are we to understand this experience in which God in Jesus Christ lays hold of us and changes the center of life from self to God?

We have to think of it in terms of human analogies, and these are very limited. We do have mechanical analogies: A man, for example, drives a nail into a wall. Some people think of predestination in this way, as though human beings were things, nails to be driven into a wall.

But there are also personal analogies. Since to be human is to be a person, and since it is our faith that whatever else God may be, he is at least personal, we are most likely to understand predestination rightly when we think of it in terms of personal analogies. John Calvin declared that in this matter of predestination God does not deal with us as sticks or stones but as persons. Augustine once said that a person who never had a friend could never understand faith. Friendship is more like faith than anything else in human experience.[7]

If there is any clue in human experience as to the nature of predestination, it is to be found in the deepest of those experiences, friendship and love. Whenever a person falls in love—that is, if he or she loves very deeply—there is always something in the life of the person loved that reaches out and elicits love. You simply do not fall in love by making up your mind that you are going to fall in love. There is always something about the person loved that calls forth love. And yet love is called forth in such a way as to do no violence to our own will. We love freely. In fact, we are never so free as when we do the will of the person whom we love. But love can never be explained in terms of our own will.

In Christopher Fry's play *The Dark Is Light Enough,* the Countess explains why she never fell in love:

> I mean, simply,
> It never came about.
> There we have no free-will.
> At the one place of experience
> Where we're most at mercy, and where
> The decision will alter us to the end of our days,
> Our destination is fixed;
> *We're elected into love.*[8]

Predestination means that the love of God in the life, death, and resurrection of Jesus Christ reaches forth and lays hold of us perhaps in the nurture of youth, perhaps in some moment of great joy, or in the face of a decision that lays bare our soul, or in the crisis of death, and calls forth a love of God that is not selfishness but true salvation.

Now it is clear enough that what has been said does not solve the mystery of those who reject the love of God. Some Calvinist theologians eliminated the mystery by saying quite frankly that God passed over them and left them to their just fate. This solves the mystery, but it is difficult to reconcile with the clear assertion of the New Testament that God desires the salvation of all people, as well as with the revelation of the love of God in Jesus Christ. For this reason many prefer to leave the problem of those who reject God as a mystery. We do not know how or why it is that the love of God can be rejected. We do know that when we reject God the cause is within us, and that when we turn to God we do so because he first laid hold of us.

William Temple has said that when we are close to God we emphasize what he has done for us, but when we stand a long way from God we must focus attention upon what we have done and what we can do. Admittedly, our ultimate relation to God is beyond our power to achieve. But some things we can do. We can resolve each day to think about Jesus Christ, what he said and what he did; we can seek to do his will; we can take our place in the fellowship of his people. The things we can do are not inconsiderable; and if we do them, it is more likely that we shall know the miracle of divine grace which is beyond our power.[9]

Predestination is a doctrine that belongs at the end, not at the beginning, of the Christian life. In writing his systematic theology, Calvin experimented with the location of the doctrine of predestination. In the final edition of the *Institutes* he located it after the doctrine of salvation and just before the doctrine of resurrection. This location seems to suggest that the doctrine stands not at the beginning of the Christian life but at the end, when Christians look back over their Christian experience and exclaim, "This is what God has done in and through my life!" This is the testimony of all the great saints. They have regarded their own lives, insofar as they were good, not as their own achievements but as the work of God's grace.

As Calvin put it, knowledge of predestination is nothing more than the testimony that we are sons of God; that is, of the grace and mercy of God. And in the presence of that grace we can but exclaim, "O the depth of the riches and wisdom and knowledge of God! How unsearchable are his judgments and how inscrutable his ways! For who has known the mind of the Lord, or who has been his counselor? ... For from him and through him and to him are all things. To him be glory for ever. Amen" (Rom. 11:33–34, 36).

Vocation

We are not only chosen by God, we are called to serve God. In the Reformed tradition, this always meant that our election is not simply to the ultimate destinies of heaven and hell but to the embodiment of the purposes of God here and now in time and space. Paul Scherer, the great Lutheran preacher, once said that the joy of religion is not in being good. People get bored and tired with being good. The joy of religion is trusting God in the presence of some great darkness and waiting for the light to break.[10] No Calvinist could have said it better. The joy of religion is embodying, at least in a broken and fragmentary way, the purposes of the eternal God in the ordinary events of our sometimes ordinary lives. Our Christian vocation, as the Reformed theologians understood this and other New Testament passages, is not simply to sanctification but also to a work. God has called us not simply to be but also to do, to work in his creation.

The work to which God calls us is not distinctively Christian. In fact, there is no distinctively Christian work.[11] The work to which God calls us is the work that is available to every human being. A Christian work may be any work that enhances human life, serves human needs, and glorifies the Creator. Christians for the most part do the same work that non-Christians do. The difference is not in the work but in the faith, in the disposition, and in the sense of accountability that Christians bring to the task. Christians do their work as those who trust in God: that is, as those who know that the final salvation of life is not in their work but in God. Hence Christians can do their work without falling, on the one hand, into despair or, on the other hand, into a fanaticism that takes work too seriously. The Christian knows that in the end, as we commit our persons to the care of God, we also have to commit unto God's care the work that we do.

Christians are distinguished by the disposition they bring to their work. The Christian works with an openness to the neighbor, a humaneness, a readiness to forgive.

Finally, Christians do their work as those who know that they are responsible: that is, that they are accountable to God for the time and energy that he has entrusted to their stewardship.

The work Christians do is not noticeably different from the work non-Christians do. The difference lies in the faith, the disposition, the accountability. It also lies in the Christian conviction that one's work is a vocation: that is, a calling. The word "vocation" survives in our secular culture, but most people who use it would have a difficult time defining who is doing the calling. Christians live with the faith that they are called to their work by the Creator of heaven and earth, by the God and Father of our Lord Jesus Christ. In one of the most remarkable sentences in the *Institutes of the Christian Religion,* John Calvin declares that this awareness that we are called by God to our work transforms the humblest task into something that is very precious in the sight of God.[12]

Sanctified

God has chosen us to be holy. The Christian life is not only forgiveness but also sanctification. "We cannot say more of the Holy Spirit and his work than that he is the power in which Jesus Christ attests himself effectively, creating in man response and obedience."[13] The Holy Spirit awakens, enlightens, and quickens. Sanctification is the outworking in concrete human life of our election before the foundation of the world. It is the human end of everything God has done for our salvation, that a human life should be restored in the image of God, that human life should become what God made it to be, that we should grow "to mature manhood, to the measure of the stature of the fulness of Christ" (Eph. 4:13).

Sanctification is a work of God and a human work, a work in which we participate. From one perspective, sanctification is wholly the work of God. From the perspective of the historical and the psychological, it is wholly a human work. Moreover, for some, sanctification is a work that moves gradually from birth to death. For others, it is full of drama and crises. Holding together sanctification as God's work and a human work, a slow, gradual development and a life of dramatic crises, requires more skill than many congregations can manage. Few congregations in actual practice hold forth the full possibilities of becoming a new person in Christ.

The important factor is that sanctification is the Christian calling and the Christian hope. When the church loses this hope that life can be transformed, the heart has gone out of faith. This optimism of

grace that life can be transformed, so powerful in the preaching of
a Wesley and the perfectionist groups, seems mute today in many
established churches. Yet it is significant that congregations and
denominations which promise the possibility of radical conversion
are now among those with the greatest increase in membership. It
is also worth noting that as ethical reflection has increased in many
churches, there has been a decrease in concern with sanctification in
individual life on the congregational level. Furthermore, the
denominations that appear to be most optimistic about changing the
policies of great nations, as well as economic and social systems, seem
less concerned and optimistic about the possibility of significant
transformation of the life of individuals in the congregation. Yet it is
just this hope that human life, the concrete life of individuals, can be
transformed and moved from darkness to light that is the consistent
message of the New Testament.

Our pessimism about the possibilities of transforming human life
can be easily understood. The lives of many Christians do not significantly differ from the lives of non-Christians. The recalcitrance of
human life to renewal and transformation once it has been set by
many years of practice or become addicted to drugs is obvious. Yet
human lives do change under the power of the Holy Spirit. In many
churches, the witness to this transforming power occurs in dramatic
conversions. In some church situations, the growth of character takes
place below the level of observation. The human self grows under
the unobserved influence of the Holy Spirit through the means of
grace in the fellowship of the Christian church. More often than we
know, hate is changed into love, doubt and fear into trust, deceit into
integrity. Persons do grow, not simply in their capacity to love but
in the power of imagining how love acts creatively in particular
situations. Lives do grow in their capacity to detach themselves from
things, to make use of this world's goods without becoming addicted
to their necessity. Human beings do grow in their capacity to trust
God as well as to love their neighbor, to commit all that they are and
do into the keeping of God.[14]

To boast of sanctification is to lose it. Hence there is a wholesome
reticence about being holy. Yet modesty must not obscure the fact
that we are called to holiness, and in remarkable degrees people
achieve holiness under the power of the Holy Spirit in the fellowship
of the church. In any case, in the life of the church we live not by
the pessimism that may grow out of particular experiences but by the
enthusiastic promises of the New Testament that those who are in
Jesus Christ become new creatures.

The content of sanctification cannot be defined with precision
because of the freedom of the Holy Spirit and the freedom of the

human self. It has been understood as the imitation of Christ, as the freedom of a new person in Christ, as the vision of God, as obedience to the law of God. These images can both enlarge and restrict the meaning of sanctification. For example, those who conceive of the Christian life as obedience to the law of God may have the strength of a sure direction, but they may also become legalists who confuse God's laws with the laws of their culture and who lack the creativity to handle complex new moral crises. Others have understood the Christian life in less specific terms, which allow for the freedom of the self and the freedom of God as the obligated life, or the responsible life, or the answering life.

Certain qualities of the sanctified life, however, are clear. To be sanctified is first to trust God, living with the faith, serenity, and dignity of those who know this world as the creation of the God who made us and redeemed us. It is, second, a humane life, open to the neighbor and ready to forgive. It is, third, a life that knows its accountability, its answerability, not only to the self and neighbor but also to God. A fourth quality of the sanctified life is growth in the capacity to detach oneself from the things and enterprises of earth without denying their goodness. As Paul put it, whether we live or die we are the Lord's (Rom. 14:8). Being the Lord's gives a capacity to suffer deprivation without despair and affluence without arrogance. On another occasion Paul expressed this capacity for detachment even more dramatically:

> I mean, brethren, the appointed time has grown very short; from now on, let those who have wives live as though they had none, and those who mourn as though they were not mourning, and those who rejoice as though they were not rejoicing, and those who buy as though they had no goods, and those who deal with the world as though they had no dealings with it. For the form of this world is passing away.
>
> (1 Corinthians 7:29–31)

John Calvin, who emphasized that forgiveness was for the sake of sanctification and that our election is not for privilege but to service and holiness, conceived of the Christian life as the fulfillment of the purposes of God. The Christian life is not only the personal relation of a self to God, it is also the life of a self in history and in society. The Christian life has significance far beyond the individual, for it has to do with what God is doing in history.

Calvin sought to establish in Geneva the holy commonwealth, and wherever the Calvinists went they carried this vision. They sought to build in England's green and pleasant land the New Jerusalem, and those who settled in Massachusetts went on an errand into the wilderness to demonstrate to the decaying Christian community in Europe the possibility of a Christian society. The Christian life as fulfillment of the purposes of God in society is a greater possibility in some times and places than in others. How this vision can be fulfilled in a secular and pluralistic society is not yet clear. In a closed and oppressive society the possibility of fulfilling God's purposes in history becomes more remote. Hence the fulfillment of one's Christian vocation may of necessity be very personal, but the vision of the holy community as well as the holy life must be maintained.

Calvin insisted that the glory of God is more important than the salvation of one's own soul. Hence Calvinists were always skeptical of those who became preoccupied with the salvation of their own souls or the preciousness of their own holiness. Calvin would be even less content with the secularized versions of saving one's own soul that are prevalent today; for example, the realization of one's potential. Nicholas Berdyaev gives a horrible account of saints who are ready to trample over each other getting through the narrow gates of heaven.[15] Sanctification has to do with personal life, but it always directs personal life away from the self, away even from its own holiness, to the fulfillment of the purposes of God in history and society. God has chosen us not simply to the ultimate destiny of heaven but to serve him in the world.

This discussion of sanctification as certain qualities or activities or images of life must not obscure the fact that sanctification has to do with the human soul, or what we would call today the self or the I. John Calvin never speculated about the nature of the soul, in part because he had no doubt about his own identity as a soul or self and in part because he knew that self is finally a mystery. A. A. Hodge defined the soul as the self, or the I, of which we are immediately conscious and which expresses itself through the body.[16] Sanctification for Calvin was the transformation of the self, the person, so that the energies, vitalities, affections, and intentions of the self were oriented toward God. This unification of the self, this establishment of the identity of the self, the I, takes place by God's grace and the activities of the self which shape the self. The self grows and establishes its identity, its character, as the self believes, worships, and acts. Calvin insisted, and Jonathan Edwards later emphasized, that in sanctification human affections play an important role, together with the mind and the will. Sanctification is not simply mental assent to a proposition, nor is it legal obedience; it is an affection. Sanctification gives a new orientation to the mind, the will, the affection; it gives to the Christian person an identity or a character by which relationships with the world and other human beings are determined and from which actions flow. Above all, it is an orientation of the self toward God, as Creator, Judge, and Redeemer, making the glory of God the chief end of life.

The gospel is God's calling us to be "holy and blameless before him in love" (Eph. 1:4, RSV margin). Our task in the church is to be alive to this possibility for every human life.

Eternal Life

Calvinists have always found confidence in the assurance that God "destined us in love to be his sons through Jesus Christ, according to the purpose of his will, to the praise of his glorious grace which he freely bestowed on us in the Beloved" (Eph. 1:5–6). This has given Christian people a poise and a dignity in the face of what appears to be inevitable defeat and destruction. The brutalities, the absurdities, the obvious destruction round about us tempt us all to believe that life itself is the product of forces with no prevision of their end, and its destiny is a universe in ruins.

The ambiguity of the human situation is nowhere more clearly expressed than in Paul's declaration that "our commonwealth is in heaven, and from it we await a Savior, the Lord Jesus Christ, who will change our lowly body to be like his glorious body" (Phil. 3:20–21). The New Testament is everywhere moved by the conviction that this world of flesh and blood is not the only world there is. Furthermore, this world is not the most important world.

There is an order of existence at work in this world of flesh and blood, yet not enclosed or bound to nature and history, which moves by the power of God to its fulfillment in his eternal kingdom.

The Christian hope is twofold, as expressed so clearly by Paul in his letter to the Philippians. On the one hand, Paul can say, "For to me to live is Christ, and to die is gain. If it is to be life in the flesh, that means fruitful labor for me. Yet which I shall choose I cannot tell. I am hard pressed between the two. My desire is to depart and be with Christ, for that is far better. But to remain in the flesh is more necessary on your account" (Phil. 1:21–24). Here Paul anticipates that at death life will continue with Christ, a hope which is presupposed on every page of the New Testament and on every page of the *Institutes of the Christian Religion.*

Yet Paul's hope is not simply eternal life for himself but the consummation of all things by the power of God. He looks forward to the time "that at the name of Jesus every knee should bow, in heaven and on earth and under the earth, and every tongue confess that Jesus Christ is Lord, to the glory of God the Father" (Phil. 2:10–11). At no point are contemporary culture and much of contemporary religion so out of concord, not only with the *Institutes of the Christian Reli-*

gion but also with the New Testament. The silence of contemporary theology about either eternal life or the consummation of all things by God is pervasive. On the other hand, there are those who openly declare that they see no hope for eternal life and even regard it as a possible handicap to Christian religion.

The hope of eternal life is one of the oldest and most pervasive of all human ideas. Until the contemporary theological period, it was openly and forthrightly at the heart of Christian faith. Eternal life, Walter Lowrie once wrote, is the core doctrine that brings all Christian doctrines into systematic coherence. " 'This is the Christian faith, apart from which, without doubt, a man must perish everlastingly.' These words, which sound astonishing and offensive when used as an introduction to the subtleties of the so-called Athanasian Creed, do not seem unreasonable when applied to belief in eternal life."[17] In our own day, an impressive witness has been given by George Kennan, for many years the representative of our country in the Soviet Union. He was deeply impressed by the dreariness of a Soviet funeral, in which the meaninglessness of life was expounded by the meaninglessness of death. In a remarkable paragraph, Ambassador Kennan, a devout Christian, bears this testimony:

> As an adequate and enduring personal philosophy Marxism has many deficiencies; but the greatest of them is that it has, in contrast to Christianity, no answer to the phenomenon of death. This is why there is nothing more pathetic than a Marxist funeral; for to the Marxists this formality celebrates nothing more than an inexplicable, unpreventable, and profoundly discouraging event in the human experience. Unable to give meaning to death, Marxism is unable to give meaning to life. This helplessness is the guarantee of its impermanence and ultimate failure as a personal and political ideology.[18]

The Christian hope in the presence of death is not simply for survival. Eternal life refers primarily to quality of life, of which duration is only one dimension. Furthermore, duration is more than clock time, one thing after another. The nature of eternal life is a mystery and hope. Yet we have some understanding of the eternal by the power of the human self to transcend temporality through memory and anticipation. We also have some knowledge of the quality of eternal life from its present reality. "This is eternal life, that they know thee the only true God, and Jesus Christ whom thou hast sent" (John 17:3). In this life Christians are a new creation, have risen with Christ and experienced the kingdom of God as righteousness, peace, and joy in the Holy Spirit (Rom. 14:17). The Christian hope cannot be separated from the present experience, which belongs in its fruition to the hope. Furthermore, the doctrine of the resurrection of the

body has always distinguished the Christian hope from any understanding of immortality that minimized the individual historical life.
The resurrection of the body means that the life which is lived in
time and space and expressed through the body will be both judged
and fulfilled beyond death. Critics contend that hope of life beyond
death is egocentricity, but this is not the Christian hope that is portrayed in the New Testament. The death of the Christian is not a fate
which overwhelms but an act in which the believer participates as
well as the church in the committal, the handing over to the keeping
of the God and Father of our Lord Jesus Christ one's lifework and the
fate of conscious personality itself.

The God who chose us before the foundation of the world and
destined us to be his sons is the foundation for the declaration of our
faith in the Nicene Creed: "I look for the resurrection of the dead;
and the life of the world to come." This is the Christian witness which
the church made in the New Testament and continued to make in
good times and bad right up to modern times. And this is the Christian witness today.

William Temple put the dilemma for those who would deny this
witness in this way:

> For man's moral and spiritual life is in this world a baffled and thwarted
> enterprise; and the scene of our endeavor is slowly becoming uninhabit-
> able, so that even though men labor for a remote posterity, yet if this
> life only is permitted them, it will one day make no difference whether
> we have striven or not for noble causes and lofty ideals. An earth as cold
> as the moon will revolve about a dying sun. Duty and love will have lost
> their meaning.[19]

For the Christian tradition, the hope of immortality was a necessary
consequence of faith in God. The tradition also bears witness that the
Christian hope has been corrupted by all forms of human selfishness.
Yet without the hope, as Austin Farrer plainly says, Christian faith no
longer makes sense.[20] The loss of intelligibility may be obscured in
secular communities, but it is not likely to be obscured for long in the
worshiping, believing congregation. If George Kennan is right that
a social movement such as communism cannot finally succeed because it has no answer for the problem of death, this is even more
true of a religion, and especially a faith which proclaims a way of life
that cannot be justified on the plane of history. As the old proverb
put it, a live dog is always better than a dead lion.

The gospel that God thought of us before we were and elected us
to be his people gives depth and meaning to human life. When this
faith is embodied in life it produces strong, self-determining persons,

a quality of human life that some think Rembrandt captured in his portraits. Paul Tillich found, in such portraits as that of Jan Six, strong, lonely, tragic, but unbroken persons, "carrying the marks of their unique histories in every line of their faces, expressing the ideals of personality of a humanistic Protestantism."[21] Leon Wencelius, a Calvin scholar, concludes that the portrait of Jan Six embodies the drama of predestination.[22] The person chosen before the foundation of the world does not live on the surface waves of history and nature, despite the buffeting of these waves. The life of such a person is rooted in the will and purposes of the creator, and this depth of existence shows in one's face.

6

A New Heaven
and a New Earth

The Bible begins with the question of human origin, and it ends with the question of human destiny. In between, the mystery of the human self, its power for self-reflection and for freedom, raises questions about the significance of human life in history. The mystery of the universe and the human self are alike placed by the Bible in the context of the greater mystery of God's freedom and mercy.

The New Testament makes the stupendous assertion that Jesus Christ is both the beginning of the created order and its end. "All things were made through him, and without him was not anything made that was made" (John 1:3). "He is before all things, and in him all things hold together" (Col. 1:17). "For he [God] has made known to us in all wisdom and insight the mystery of his will, according to his purpose which he set forth in Christ as a plan for the fulness of time, to unite all things in him, things in heaven and things on earth" (Eph. 1:9–10).

Human beings, if magazine articles are an indication, choose to speculate about human origins rather than human destiny.[1] This is somewhat strange, for human destiny is a more existential question. Yet the great debate in public school education centers, for example, on the origin of the universe, not on the future of the universe. It may be that on the less intellectually sophisticated theological levels of discussion, the destiny of the universe is the center of attention, as the popularity of such books as *The Late Great Planet Earth* would substantiate.[2] However, in universities and in magazines that appeal to university people, discussion of the end of the universe pales into insignificance compared to discussions of the origin.

The possibility of a nuclear holocaust has awakened attention. Yet for all its incredible horror, the nuclear holocaust is more manageable and susceptible to human intentions than our ultimate human destiny. The final destiny of the world relativizes even so horrible a historical event as a nuclear holocaust. It is at least possible that human beings can avoid a nuclear war, or that at least some can survive, though there is little in history to provide long-term hopes on either point. The fact is that the future of the human race is very precarious even apart from a nuclear holocaust. The evidence seems to indicate that the human race on this planet will someday come to an end, leaving no memory that it ever was. Human destiny apart from the providence of God seems to be subject to blind fate or caprice.

Artists and poets have been better able than philosophers and theologians to face the ultimate destiny. This was true of Renaissance artists such as Albrecht Dürer (1471–1528), who pictured the last judgment as a final summing up of human history. John Milton and John Bunyan likewise knew that life moved toward a divine judgment. In our own time, T. S. Eliot concluded that the world ends not with a bang but with a whimper.[3] W. B. Yeats, in one of the most moving poems of the twentieth century, "The Second Coming," aware of the disintegration of life, first expects the Christian revelation, the Second Coming, but replaces it with a "figure of gross unreason and mindless violence."[4]

The question of destiny will not go away, even though we are obviously more comfortable talking about human origin. What does human life amount to in the end? What can we hope for? We can, of course, take other attitudes toward the future. We can fear the future, be anxious about the future, be resigned to the future, be distracted from thinking about the future. But something in human nature compels us to hope, as Browning put it:

> One who never turned his back but marched breast forward,
> Never doubted clouds would break,
> Never dreamed, though right were worsted, wrong would triumph,
> Held we fall to rise, are baffled to fight better.
> Sleep to wake.[5]

Human hope has two dimensions. The first is individual. What happens to the human person, the individual, the I? Each person's historical end comes in death. The question simply put is, Is there something beyond death? Over against the problem of individual death, the Christian faith gives the hope of eternal life, as discussed in chapter 5.

The other dimension to hope is social. No person is simply an individual. Each person shares in a history and in a society. Each person's destiny is social as well as individual. Therefore the question of human hope has to include the end of human societies, even of the universe itself. What is the final history of nations, societies, and cultures? This is an individual question as well as a social question, for each individual participates in a state, a society, and a culture. An individual's destiny includes the history of which the individual was a part.

The question of human hope, therefore, raises at least three questions. What is the destiny of the human person? What is possible in human life and in human history? Finally, what is the destiny, not only of the individual but also of human history and of the universe itself?

The answers to these questions must of necessity be modest. The fact that we are creatures limited by time and space means that we do not have any final knowledge of the future. Even in science, the physicist cannot predict the course of a falling leaf, much less the future history of the physical universe. History is further complicated by human freedom. Moreover, there is the ultimate mystery of what lies beyond the brackets that encompass the universe. We cannot get outside the universe, as it were, and see it as observers. Hence any speculation about the future must be very sober.

The response of Christian faith to our human situation is finally based on what we know of God. Our knowledge of the future is shaped by the way we believe God has worked in creation and redemption. More specifically, the commitment of faith concerning the future is based on what we know about God in Jesus Christ, on our conviction that Jesus Christ whom we know in history stands at the end of history as its Lord and judge.

In the last chapter, the Christian hope for the individual in personal sanctification and life beyond death was discussed. In this chapter, our concern is with the Christian hope in its social dimensions and in relation to life in history. The life of the Christian in society, especially as the Christian faces the future, can be discussed in the context of three questions: (1) What is the dominant image or metaphor that the Christian has for life in history? (2) What is possible in human history? (3) How shall human history come to an end? These three questions do not address all the problems, but answers to them, however provisional, do provide an orientation by which Christians can live in the contemporary world.

The Christian as Resident Alien

The Christian lives in this world, Augustine of Hippo concluded in the maturity of his life, as a resident alien.[6] As a resident, the Christian takes pride in earthly achievements and is responsible not only for the stewardship of earth but for the proper ordering of society. As an alien, the Christian knows that his or her life is not defined by this world: that is, by the world we can see, taste, touch, and handle. The Christian knows that this is not the only world there is, and that however significant it may be, it is not the most important world. In this world of nature and history, there is another order of existence, not bound by nature and history, that moves to its completion in God's eternal kingdom.

This is an ancient theme, which is repeatedly affirmed in the New Testament. Jesus himself said, "Do not lay up for yourselves treasures on earth, where moth and rust consume and where thieves break in and steal, but lay up for yourselves treasures in heaven, where neither moth nor rust consumes and where thieves do not break in and steal. For where your treasure is, there will your heart be also" (Matt. 6:19–21). Paul declared, "Our commonwealth is in heaven, and from it we await a Savior, the Lord Jesus Christ, who will change our lowly body to be like his glorious body, by the power which enables him even to subject all things to himself" (Phil. 3:20–21). The writer of 1 Peter beseeched his hearers as aliens and exiles to abstain from the passions of this world.

In the early church, the *Letter to Diognetus* carries on this tradition with singular clarity.

> For Christians cannot be distinguished from the rest of the human race by country, or language, or customs. They do not live in cities of their own; they do not use a peculiar form of speech; they do not follow an eccentric manner of life. . . . They live in their own countries, but only as aliens. They have a share in everything as citizens, and endure everything as foreigners. Every foreign land is their fatherland, and yet for them every fatherland is a foreign land. They marry, like everyone else, and they beget children, but they do not cast out their offspring. They share their board with each other, but not their marriage bed. . . . they love all men, and by all men are persecuted. . . . they are poor, yet they make many rich; they are completely destitute, yet they enjoy complete abundance. . . . What the soul is in the body, that Christians are in the world. . . . The soul is shut up in the body, and yet itself holds the body together; while Christians are restrained in the world as in a prison, and yet themselves hold the world together.[7]

This conviction that Christians are resident aliens contributed to the antagonism between the Roman empire and the Christian community in the last half of the third century and the beginning of the fourth.[8] In the earlier centuries the empire had regarded Christians more or less as a nuisance and had dealt with them by police action. By the middle of the third century, it was becoming clear that the Christian community and the Roman empire were mutually exclusive. The Christians believed that the meaning of life was found in Jesus Christ as Lord and Savior. The Romans, who were also a mes-

sianic community, believed that life had been fulfilled in the achievements of Caesar Augustus and in participation in the rationally ordered society of Rome. The piety of Vergil's *Aeneid* gave profound
expression to the faith that human life could be fulfilled in the political, social, and economic achievements of Rome. Rome was the destined town and Caesar Augustus was the child of promise. Even after
the empire had recognized Christians under Constantine and had
become officially Christian under Theodosius, the old Romans clung
to their faith and regarded Christianity as somehow subversive of the
social order. The piety of Aeneas and the piety of the Christian were
finally exclusive. Augustine, in his younger years, had shared something of Eusebius's vision of the Christian empire as the climax of
history. "The whole world," as Augustine sang, "has become a choir
praising our Christ."[9] In his older years, Augustine came to see that
eternal Rome was eternal nonsense. Human security is to be found
not in any social, political, or economic order, however noble, but in
God. The political, economic, and social orders come and go. On the
one hand, they represent remarkable achievements of human wisdom, of human goodness, and of the freedom of the human spirit.
And on the other hand, these achievements are fragile, limited by
time and space and human energy and corrupted by human sin.
Every human achievement, Augustine knew, is an ordinate good
which must not be loved inordinately. When citizens of the empire
flocked into Augustine's cathedral in 410 after the fall of Rome,
Augustine comforted them by reminding them of their first identity
as citizens of Jerusalem. Augustine, as a good Roman, was proud of
Rome's achievements, but as a Christian, he knew they were not only
finite and limited but corrupted by human sin. The final meaning of
life is to be found not in any city of earth but in the city of God.
Augustine expressed his conviction that the Christian is a resident
alien in remarkable paragraphs of the great nineteenth book of the
City of God.

> But a household of human beings whose life is not based on faith is in
> pursuit of an earthly peace based on the things belonging to this tempo-
> ral life, and on its advantages, whereas a household of human beings
> whose life is based on faith looks forward to the blessings which are
> promised as eternal in the future, making use of earthly and temporal
> things like a pilgrim in a foreign land, who does not let himself be taken
> in by them or distracted from his course towards God, but rather treats
> them as supports which help him more easily to bear the burdens of
> "the corruptible body which weighs heavy on the soul"; they must on
> no account be allowed to increase the load. Thus both kinds of men and
> both kinds of households alike make use of the things essential for this
> mortal life; but each has its own very different end in making use of

them. So also the earthly city, whose life is not based on faith, aims at an earthly peace, and it limits the harmonious agreement of citizens concerning the giving and obeying of orders to the establishment of a kind of compromise between human wills about the things relevant to mortal life. In contrast, the Heavenly City—or rather that part of it which is on pilgrimage in this condition of mortality, and which lives on the basis of faith—must needs make use of this peace also, until this mortal state, for which this kind of peace is essential, passes away. And therefore, it leads what we may call a life of captivity in this earthly city as in a foreign land, although it has already received the promise of redemption, and the gift of the Spirit as a kind of pledge of it; and yet it does not hesitate to obey the laws of the earthly city by which those things which are designed for the support of this mortal life are regulated; and the purpose of this obedience is that, since this mortal condition is shared by both cities, a harmony may be preserved between them in things that are relevant to this condition. . . .

While this Heavenly City, therefore, is on pilgrimage in this world, she calls out citizens from all nations and so collects a society of aliens, speaking all languages. She takes no account of any difference in customs, laws, and institutions, by which earthly peace is achieved and preserved—not that she annuls or abolishes any of those, rather, she maintains them and follows them (for whatever divergences there are among the diverse nations, those institutions have one single aim— earthly peace), provided that no hindrance is presented thereby to the religion which teaches that the one supreme and true God is to be worshipped. Thus even the Heavenly City in her pilgrimage here on earth makes use of the earthly peace and defends and seeks the compromise between human wills in respect of the provisions relevant to the mortal nature of man, so far as may be permitted without detriment to true religion and piety. In fact, that City relates the earthly peace to the heavenly peace, which is so truly peaceful that it should be regarded as the only peace deserving the name, at least in respect of the rational creation; for this peace is the perfectly ordered and completely harmonious fellowship in the enjoyment of God, and of each other in God. When we arrive at that state of peace, there will be no longer a life that ends in death, but a life that is life in sure and sober truth; there will be no animal body to "weigh down the soul" in its process of corruption; there will be a spiritual body with no cravings, a body subdued in every part to the will. This peace the Heavenly City possesses in faith while on its pilgrimage, and it lives a life of righteousness, based on this faith, having the attainment of that peace in view to every good action it performs in relation to God, and in relation to a neighbour, since the life of a city is inevitably a social life.[10]

Contemporary American Christianity has been thoroughly indoctrinated in the responsibility of the church for the world. This is a genuine responsibility. The church exists in the world as a sacrament, an outward and visible sign of what God intends the human community to be. It is in the world to serve the world, not to be served by the world. This lesson has been learned very well by modern churches. Yet the result has been not so much the Christianization of society as the secularization of the church.

The secularization of the church is nowhere better seen than in the doctrine of the ministry. Forty years ago, churches *called* ministers. Moreover, the church believed that God also called pastors to particular churches and responsibilities. Today, the church has adopted the personnel policies of American corporations so that there is little difference between hiring a minister and hiring a manager for any American business. We have come so far as to speak of executives and even of chief executive officers in the church and its institutions, though there is no executive, much less chief executive, mentioned in the New Testament. Whereas, a hundred years ago, Presbyterians spoke of the crown rights of the Redeemer in the life of the church, we now talk about management and process. The problem in the church is no longer an awareness of the church's responsibility for the world. Indeed, that responsibility preoccupies every General Assembly and an overwhelming amount of staff work. The forgotten note in the life of the church is that the Christian community is a colony of heaven, that the Christian's first citizenship is not in the societies of earth but in the kingdom of God. Furthermore, the service the church renders is frequently little different from that of political parties and other special-interest groups. It is often forgotten that the church's first and greatest service to the world is to preach the gospel of Jesus Christ.

Augustine's conviction that the Christian is a resident alien enabled him to face the fall of Rome with great sorrow and regret, but not with utter despair. He never believed that human security and finally salvation rested in Rome. This truth about human life and human societies was put with dramatic power by Emil Brunner in an address at Yale University Divinity School in 1947. Emil Brunner declared that the United States of America was perhaps the greatest achievement of the human spirit in the history of the human race, but, he added, there will come a day when the United States will no longer exist. When that day comes, he said, each one of you will still be. Hence, what happens in the history of a human soul is in some way more important than what happens in the history of a great society.[11]

The metaphor of resident alien enabled a great theologian and a great Roman such as Augustine to appreciate the achievements of Rome, on the one hand, and on the other hand to know that the Christian community's final destiny is not Rome but the City of God. In every age, this understanding of the Christian life has enabled the church to be responsible in the world and yet not of the world. In this world, the Christian is at one and the same time a resident and an alien. The Christian's final citizenship is in heaven.

What Is Possible in History?

The question remains, What is possible in human history? The resident alien is still resident in this society and in this history. What can be achieved in history is important to the individual and to the whole human race. The answer to the question of what is possible in human history determines in significant measure how a Christian lives in the political, social, economic, and cultural orders. Much of the debate about political, economic, and social policies, and much of the confusion about church pronouncements, arises out of different understandings of what is possible in history.

Many people, including some Christians, have not believed that any really significant achievements are possible in history. Therefore they have been resigned to live as best they can and hope for salvation by escape from this world of flesh and blood and tears. They sometimes withdraw from the world and establish their own communities, as in the case of some Protestant sects, as well as the monastic orders of Catholicism. The pessimists have generally emphasized not only the limitations of creatureliness but, in particular, the limitations of human sin. In some situations, as in closed and coercive societies, this pessimistic response is the only historical possibility.

Others are very optimistic about the possibilities of human history. They are confident about the resources of human reason or of religion to manage the impulses of nature and the disorders of society. They have usually believed that the basic human problem inheres in bad structures and social orders. They have been confident that when reason has been brought to bear upon these structures and the social order devised according to the principles of justice, the good society is possible. They have quiet confidence in political action and the appropriation of money. They generally have little awareness that the possibilities of political life and economic productivity are significantly determined by religion, culture, and history. The optimists have usually minimized human problems such as greed or self-centeredness or pride and emphasized the significance of social planning.

The answer to the question of what is possible in history can lead on the one hand to cynicism, to despair, to a feeling of helplessness. On the other hand, an optimistic answer to the question can lead to the fanaticism of those who know the truth and who are sure that by planning they can establish the ideal society. Each answer is abundantly illustrated in history. In recent years, under the influence of liberation theologies, theologies of hope, and political theologies, many Christians have become increasingly optimistic about what is possible in the future. The proper orientation of the Christian life is toward the future which God is bringing to pass. The tremendous achievements of modern science, in particular developments of liberal political democracies in western Europe and in the United States, as well as the enormous economic productivity of Western society, have all conspired to encourage human hopes for the future.

The historical answers of Reformed theology to the question of what is possible in human history satisfy neither the optimist nor the pessimist. When the human situation is viewed from the perspective of Reformed theology, the outlook is one of a Christian realism that gives in neither to despair on the one hand nor to utopian hopes on the other. It sets no boundaries about what may be achieved in the future, but it knows of no reason to believe that future historical achievements will be of a different order from achievements in the past. The possibilities of human history are limited by human finiteness and also by human sinfulness. Furthermore, all human achievements are not simply related to discrete acts of the will or to legislative pronouncements but are deeply rooted in culture, in history, and in religion. Every vision of the future must take seriously the nature of a human being and the involvement of human beings in cultures, histories, and religions which develop over centuries and out of movements which can neither be planned nor legislated nor bought with money.

The New Testament nowhere promises that love will ever be triumphant in history. The actual writings of the New Testament indicate that, in history, love will always be crucified love. There is no suggestion in the New Testament that the Christian life can ever be justified by history. There are partial justifications of Christian commitment in history, but these remain fragmentary. As Reinhold Niebuhr insisted, sacrificial love can never be justified within history.[12] For within history, a live dog is always better than a dead lion.

Christian realism, which moves between despair and utopianism, is based upon two convictions.[13] The first is the permanence of the nature of the human self. The other is the prospect that God will continue to respect human freedom and act in human history as he has in the past.

The possibilities of human history are on the one hand established and on the other hand limited by the nature of a human being. Most of what Christian faith says about human beings can be put under four heads. Human beings are (1) finite creatures, limited by time, space, intelligence, energy; (2) made in the image of God; (3) broken by human sin; (4) redeemed in Christ. Each of these affirmations bears upon what is possible in human history.

Every human being is a creature. We have to be in one space, not in many spaces; in one time, not in many times. Moreover, time moves on relentlessly and is irreversible. We cannot do again what we did in the past. We can be young only once. Our human energies are finally depleted. We have just so much intellectual capacity. Finally, we die.

Instinct and impulse, which belong to human nature, sometimes defy both reason and the human will. The determination of human behavior by religion, culture, and history modifies all political and social decisions. The technical complexity of human existence means that people may starve in a world of plenty in spite of good intentions. The disaster of the space shuttle *Challenger* is a reminder that no matter now much money or technical skill may be brought to bear upon a problem, so long as human beings are in charge there is always the possibility of disaster. The created character of human existence sets limits to what is possible in history.

Human beings are also made in the image of God to reflect the divine glory. This is possible because of the unique capacities of the self, in particular the power of the human spirit. Human beings are not only conscious of the world; they are also conscious of themselves and have powers of self-reflection. The human spirit can objectify the self, pass judgment upon the self, and organize the energies and vitalities of human existence to pursue a goal, set by its perception of what the self is and of what the self should be. This gives human beings a certain freedom over instinct and impulse, over culture, and even over their past. Moreover, the power of the human spirit transcends every human act and goes beyond anything that has been achieved. No human achievement ever exhausts the possibilities of human life. There is always something more.

The powers of the human spirit and human freedom also mean that human beings have the possibilities of sin. The freedom and transcendence of the spirit give to all persons remarkable capacities for loyalty, for commitment, for sacrifice, but they also provide the power for greed, selfishness, paranoid distrust of one's neighbors, and the capacity to transmute the impulse to survive into the will to dominate. Human beings are not only impulsive and instinctual, as animals are; they can use and intensify instincts and impulses as instruments of self-centeredness. Moreover, human beings are also able to reject the conclusions of reason.

The fact that the human spirit can transcend not only the self but every human achievement means that the human spirit is never finally satisfied with any social, political, economic, or cultural order.

No society ever exhausts the possibilities of human creativity. We know there is something more. This something more is not simply the possibilities of human creativity, but also the fact that human creativity cannot finally satisfy the self. The human spirit reaches out to something that is beyond every human achievement and therefore subject to tragic frustrations whenever too much is expected of human achievements. As Augustine, the great theologian of Hippo, put it, "Thou hast made us for thyself and restless is our heart until it comes to rest in thee."[14]

The third fact about human nature from the point of view of Christian theology that significantly influences what is possible is human sinfulness. "All have sinned and fall short of the glory of God" (Rom. 3:23). The universal fact is that all human beings act out of self-interest. In many instances, self-interest is overcome to an amazing degree. It can be modified by devotion to the family, to the community, to the nation, but it lives on in the concern for my family, my community, and my nation. It is also restrained in the remarkable capacity of human beings to love and to live generously, but it lives on in the corruption of even our finest deeds by our own self-interest. As Martin Luther knew so well, we sin in our best deeds as well as our worst deeds. In retrospect we know that those deeds which once we considered virtue all seem to have been flawed by our own self-interest. Wherever human beings are, there is self-interest and there is sin.

This awareness that human beings not only are creatures of instinct and impulse but are corrupted in their freedom over instinct and impulse by self-interest convinced Reinhold Niebuhr that the possibility of a society in which love could replace force was an illusion, and that the best we can hope for is a social order in which centers of power and of self-interest are sufficiently reduced and balanced off against each other that we can have a measure of justice and freedom.[15] The human situation is such that self-interest itself must be used in the achievement of justice in society. Christians have been, as Niebuhr argued, sometimes less wise than the children of darkness in their refusal to take with sufficient seriousness the historical fact of sin which corrupts not simply the bad people but also the good people.

The cause of justice and the realization of the possibilities of the good society are hindered not simply by the sins of bad people but by the self-righteousness of the righteous. There is the self-righteousness of the successful—that is, of those who can manage their lives— who keep the law, who achieve fame, status, and fortune. There is also the self-righteousness of the reformers from the left, right, and center of the social spectrum. There is little evidence, for example, that the great reform movements of the past twenty years have had either feelings of gratitude for that which has been given to them in American society or the capacity to subject their own purposes and programs to critical evaluation. The self-assumption of establishment lobbies and reform movements alike that theirs are the causes of justice, love, and freedom precludes the possibility of constructive debate. Those who claimed to be the parties of justice, of fairness, of love are precisely those who first must be critically self-critical of their own intentions. One of Reinhold Niebuhr's greatest contributions to social ethics is his insistence that Christians must be critically self-critical in their programs, causes, and actions. A sense of contrition is a contribution that Christians should bring to the task of social justice.[16]

The powers of the human spirit to transcend the self, to reflect upon instinct and impulse, upon culture, upon one's own past, and to intend the future also mean that the possibilities for good in human society, as in human life, are indeterminate. An optimism for the future is rooted first of all in creation. Human beings were created good by a good God. Human evil is not a part of creation but an accident of history. Furthermore, evil itself is parasitic upon the good and has within its very nature the powers of self-destruction. There is a limit to what evil can accomplish. It lives upon the good and it finally destroys itself. No purely evil society, in contrast to a purely good society, can exist. There has to be honor among thieves in order for even a society of thieves to exist.

Our redemption in Christ also is related to what is possible in history. Redemption means forgiveness and sanctification. On the one hand, forgiveness undercuts the social order, putting demands of order in tension with mercy. Yet it also opens up new possibilities. Only those who have known mercy can show mercy. Sanctification also shapes society as human lives are transformed. Those within the church as well as the external critics know how slow sanctification is and how political and social actions contradict it. Yet participation in the life of the worshiping, believing community has a decisive influence on life and society. As Herbert Butterfield observed, the greatest influence of the church on the world is the indirect consequence of redemption and worship, not the result of direct action.[17] Redemption in Christ makes us aware of both the limitations and the possibilities of human history. To be redeemed in Christ is to stand under the command to be perfect and also to receive the promise of forgiveness. This redemption has social consequences.

Redemption in Christ includes the gift of the Holy Spirit. This means there is always an optimism about what may happen in a believer's life and in the church based not upon the human reality but upon the promise of the Spirit. The historical reality of lingering sin in the life of the redeemed never in the New Testament eclipses an optimism and an openness about human possibilities through the work of the Holy Spirit.

An accumulation of the means of grace is possible. A child born in a society bereft of the means of grace and a child born in the context of the means of grace begin as equals in the personal achievement of courage and of honesty. There is no way for one to inherit honesty, courage, truthfulness from one's parents or from one's society. However, birth in certain societies and in certain families places one in the context of the means of grace in which a life of truthfulness, honesty, and generosity is more likely to develop. There can be, as Arnold Toynbee saw, the possibility of an increase in the means of grace.[18]

There can be a development in the powers of the human imagination and the available images of what it is to be responsible, just, and merciful. A. D. Lindsay once said that the great difference between the saints and ordinary people is that the saints do what ordinary people never think of doing.[19] Stanley Hauerwas has written, "What is lacking is not a better moral calculus of what acts Christians should or should not do, but an enlivening of the imagination by images that do justice to the central symbols of our faith."[20] An increase in the social resources for good is a possibility.

Societies can also improve in their structures. While all structures are subject to the limitations of time and space and the frailty of the human beings who support them, they do aid or discourage acts of love, justice, and mercy. They can enhance human freedom and responsibility. No one can discount the great achievements of political democracy and economic productivity in the last few hundred years in Western society, just as one cannot depreciate the great achievements of ancient Rome and Greece.

Finally, the possibilities that are open in history are greatly enhanced by a vision of a transformed life and society. When Christians have understood that justification by faith is for the sake of sanctification, or when they have been aware of the power of the Holy Spirit to transform human life, human lives and societies have been changed for the good. The contribution of the Wesleyan revival to prison reform, to public education, to the end of slavery, and to the temperance movement is but one vivid illustration of what Christians moved by the indeterminate possibilities of the future have achieved.[21] Just as on every new level of goodness new possibilities of evil emerge, so on every new level of human social, political, and economic achievement, new possibilities of a society of justice and mercy appear.

Christian realism must be distinguished both from a pessimism that underestimates the possibilities of history and an optimism that overestimates what human beings can achieve. Hence the realist does not set any predetermined limits to what may be achieved in the cause of justice and freedom in the future. Despair, as Niebuhr taught us, is the fate of realists who know something about sin but nothing about redemption. The realist is, however, aware that on every new level of human achievement, new forms of evil appear. The Christian realist knows the technical, political, and economic complications of human life, which cannot be resolved simply by goodwill and good intentions. The human reason is finite and limited as well as corrupted by the sinful self who reasons. The realist exaggerates neither the power nor the goodness of the human reason or human will. Our human achievements are both finite and limited by our self-centeredness. Hence the Christian realist expects in the future the same order of achievements we have had in the past: partial solutions to complicated problems, some of which may never be solved; partial achievements of justice and of communities that enhance human freedom. The Christian realist also knows that every human achievement is fragile and may be destroyed by cultural, economic, and social forces as well as by human freedom.

The Christian lives in the conviction that the kingdom of God has been established in Jesus Christ and that the kingdom will come at the end of history in the fullness of its glory. In the meantime, Christians seek to achieve in the church and in society partial fulfillments of the kingdom and prepare for the time when every knee shall bow and every tongue shall confess that Jesus Christ is Lord.

The New Creation

The Bible is confident that since God created the universe, he will also bring it to its consummation. In the face of Israel's rebellion against God and the judgment of the exile in the Old Testament, as well as the crucifixion of Jesus and the dominance of the principalities and powers in the New Testament, the hope that the earth and its people will finally glorify God is never eclipsed. The covenant with Noah, with the rainbow as a symbol, was taken to mean that God will work with sinful human beings to achieve and accomplish his purposes.[22]

The vision of the fulfillment of the purposes of God in human life and history was never lost in all the discouraging history of Israel. No one has put this vision in more moving language than the writer of Isaiah 65:

> For behold, I create new heavens
>> and a new earth;
> and the former things shall not be remembered
>> or come into mind.
> But be glad and rejoice for ever
>> in that which I create;
> for behold, I create Jerusalem a rejoicing,
>> and her people a joy.
> I will rejoice in Jerusalem,
>> and be glad in my people;
> no more shall be heard in it the sound of weeping
>> and the cry of distress.
> No more shall there be in it
>> an infant that lives but a few days,
>> or an old man who does not fill out his days,
> for the child shall die a hundred years old,
>> and the sinner a hundred years old shall be accursed.
> They shall build houses and inhabit them;
>> they shall plant vineyards and eat their fruit.
> They shall not build and another inhabit;
>> they shall not plant and another eat;
> for like the days of a tree shall the days of my people be,
>> and my chosen shall long enjoy the work of their hands.
> They shall not labor in vain,
>> or bear children for calamity;
> for they shall be the offspring of the blessed of the LORD,
>> and their children with them.
> Before they call I will answer,
>> while they are yet speaking I will hear.
> The wolf and the lamb shall feed together,
>> the lion shall eat straw like the ox;
>> and dust shall be the serpent's food.
> They shall not hurt or destroy
>> in all my holy mountain,
>>>>> says the LORD.

(Isaiah 65:17–25)

These prophecies anticipated a future in history, but it is important to note that this is a future that God will bring about. The writer of the passage did not know how this good society would be achieved, but on the basis of what the prophet knew about God, he dared to envision a new heaven and a new earth.

This same vision was carried over into the New Testament. Paul looks forward not only to his being with Christ after his own death but also to the time when every knee shall bow and every tongue shall confess that Jesus Christ is Lord (Phil. 1:23; 2:9–11).

The New Testament concludes with the triumphant vision of Revelation.

> Then I saw a new heaven and a new earth; for the first heaven and the first earth had passed away, and the sea was no more. And I saw the holy city, new Jerusalem, coming down out of heaven from God, prepared as a bride adorned for her husband; and I heard a loud voice from the throne saying, "Behold, the dwelling of God is with men. He will dwell with them, and they shall be his people, and God himself will be with them; he will wipe away every tear from their eyes, and death shall be no more, neither shall there be mourning nor crying nor pain any more, for the former things have passed away."
>
> (Revelation 21:1–4)

These visions of the conclusion of human history from Isaiah and the consummation of all things from the New Testament deeply move us today, as they must have moved the Jewish exiles and the early Christians. The New Creation is affirmed in the hymns we sing.

> For all the saints who from their labors rest,
> Who thee by faith before the world confessed,
> Thy name, O Jesus, be forever blest.
> Alleluia! Alleluia!
>
> Thou wast their Rock, their Fortress, and their Might;
> Thou, Lord, their Captain in the well-fought fight;
> Thou, in the darkness drear, their one true Light.
> Alleluia! Alleluia!
>
> O may thy soldiers, faithful, true, and bold,
> Fight as the saints who nobly fought of old,
> And win with them the victor's crown of gold.
> Alleluia! Alleluia! . . .
>
> And when the fight is fierce, the warfare long,
> Steals on the ear the distant triumph song,
> And hearts are brave again, and arms are strong.
> Alleluia! Alleluia!
>
> From earth's wide bounds, from ocean's farthest coast,
> Through gates of pearl streams in the countless host,
> Singing to Father, Son, and Holy Ghost,
> Alleluia! Alleluia!

Charles Wesley's greatly loved hymn has served as a confession of faith and hope for countless Christians.

> Love divine, all loves excelling,
> Joy of heaven, to earth come down,
> Fix in us thy humble dwelling,
> All thy faithful mercies crown!
> Jesus, thou art all compassion,
> Pure, unbounded love thou art;
> Visit us with thy salvation,
> Enter every trembling heart.
>
> Finish, then, thy new creation;
> Pure and spotless let us be;
> Let us see thy great salvation
> Perfectly restored in thee;
> Changed from glory into glory,
> Till in heaven we take our place,
> Till we cast our crowns before thee,
> Lost in wonder, love, and praise.

Some Christians have understood these visions of the future in a very literal historical way. They have prepared historical narratives for the end of all things. This literal historical understanding is not possible, either in the light of what we know about the world or in the light of good exegesis. We do not have a knowledge of how history will end. The Bible does not give us this knowledge. This knowledge belongs to the future. Our hopes concerning the end of all things are determined by what we know about God from our experience and for Christians, particularly in Jesus Christ.

Christians have also understood these passages in terms of natural events as well as in terms of history. Again, the simple fact is that we do not have scientific knowledge of the natural events with which history shall be concluded. Christian affirmations about creation, about Jesus Christ, and about the consummation of all things do not provide scientific and historical information beyond what is available to scientists and historians. They do claim to provide the wisdom in the light of which nature and human history, including the history of Jesus, can be understood.

Reformed Christians, after the manner of Calvin, have viewed the future soberly and practically. In the *Institutes* Calvin had far less to say about the appearing of Jesus Christ than in his commentaries and sermons. He seemed to have assumed that for most people the end comes in death, which he understood, more matter-of-factly than Augustine, as the passage from one form of human existence to another. On the one hand, he believed, as in his commentary on Genesis 17:7, that "the renovation of the world . . . took place at the advent of Christ." But Calvin also felt the pull toward the future, commenting on Acts 3:21, "We must seek Christ no where else but

in heaven, while we wait the restoration of all things." Between the
renovation of the world in Jesus Christ and the full revelation of that
renovation in the appearing of Christ at the end, Calvin was both
busier at the task and more hopeful of what could be accomplished
in the growth of the kingdom in human history than most theologians
have been. Yet Calvin's failure to write a commentary on Revelation
could not have been accidental. He was a practical rather than a
speculative theologian. Five convictions underlay his manner of life.
(1) The renovation of the world had taken place in Jesus Christ. (2)
Speculation about the time and manner of the end is futile. (3) The
end is likely to come for us in death. (4) God is able to keep what we
have committed unto him in life and work. (5) In the meantime, we
are already engaged in the battle of Armageddon, and we ought to
be fully occupied in realizing in our history what we can of the
kingdom.

Our Christian hope is based on our knowledge of God in creation
and in redemption, particularly in Jesus Christ. On the basis of this
knowledge, the Christian hope for the future has always included the
following dimensions.

First, the Christ who became incarnate for our salvation and whom
we know in history as the crucified, risen Lord stands at the end of
history as its triumphant Lord and Judge. Everywhere in the New
Testament there is the conviction that the Christ who came will
appear at the end and will be revealed as the triumphant Lord of
history, that all powers and principalities shall acknowledge his Lordship.

Second, the end of history is always envisioned as the great assize,
the judgment of God. Good and evil, relative as they may be, do
make a difference, and in the final summing up of things, goodness
receives its reward. The judge is Christ, and the standard of his
judgment is his own life, which was crucified in history.

On the one hand, the New Testament promises forgiveness
through the blood of Christ, and on the other hand it warns of the
judgment with Christ as the judge. The two emphases have to be
held together. The final judgment means that we are responsible,
accountable, answerable before God for the lives we live. As the first
disciples, we too have to ask, Who then can be saved? The answer
is that of Jesus, "With men this is impossible, but with God all things
are possible" (Matt. 19:26). The judgment means that the pretensions
of the righteous are broken, and that the relative distinctions of good
and evil are honored. In Jesus' description of the judgment, however,
the righteous did not know that they were righteous.

A third dimension is the resurrection. In the New Testament,
resurrection includes personal immortality. Yet it gives immortality

a particular New Testament meaning. Resurrection means that God raises the dead. Human beings do not conquer death by some power inherent within the self. Furthermore, the resurrection means that the life which was expressed through the physical body is fulfilled as well as judged beyond death. The individual, the unique I, is not lost in some timeless eternity.

Fourth, the end of all things has always included the consummation of creation to the glory of God. As Christians we have no special knowledge of how the universe will end or what will happen to the natural order. The Bible persistently refers to the natural order as if something were awry, and it awaits the time when the lamb and the lion will lie down together and the mountains will praise the Lord. Beyond this hope we cannot safely go.

The Christian hope for the world has been expressed with admirable insight and soberness by the Confession of Faith (1967) of the Congregational Church in England and Wales.

> 1. *Though God's purpose for his universe is mysterious* . . . God's purpose for the physical universe is for the most part hidden from us in mystery. We do not suppose that its only purpose is the support and discipline which it provides to the bodies and minds of human beings during their lifetime on earth. We are certain that God's purpose will be worthy of his own majesty and consistent with the dignity which already appears in the splendour of the physical universe. How the universe is related to God's final and everlasting kingdom lies beyond our present possibilities of understanding. . . .
>
> 5. *Creation glorified.* We look forward to acts of God which bring final transformation to human life and admit human beings to share in his own eternal joy and felicity. The unimaginable glory of the everlasting God is the destiny for which we have been made. Cleansed from sin, we shall see God in Christ Jesus in open splendour, and he will make us like himself. We do not know in what universal framework our lives will be set; nor how, in that framework, God's other purposes for his created universe will be fulfilled. We only know that God is the source, the guide, and the goal of all that is. To him be glory for ever.[23]

The Christian hope intends to express in these four affirmations its conviction that God who created human beings and who redeemed them in Christ will bring their lives to fulfillment and to judgment. It is also the conviction that the universe itself has an enduring purpose beyond our human grasp in the intention of the Creator. The details of how the world will end are beyond our knowledge. Our conviction that God will consummate his creation is of the same order as our Christian convictions that God created the world and that God knows every human being by name, that God became incarnate in Jesus Christ for our salvation. Indeed, the Christian doctrine of the end is simply the affirmation that the God who created the world and the God who redeems his people will bring his creation and his people to fulfillment and to judgment.

The concrete existential human importance of the new heaven and earth was made vividly clear in an incident from the Second World War. Francis Pickens Miller, who for many years was secretary of the World's Student Christian Federation and a great churchman as well as statesman, was in charge of an American military unit in Germany. A lieutenant on his staff had a meeting with his Russian counterpart. The Russian asked the American lieutenant if he had read Karl Marx, to which the lieutenant replied that he had. The Russian in response said, "Then you know how it will come out." Francis Miller reflected that it would have been remarkable indeed if the lieutenant had been able to ask the Russian, "Have you read the New Testament? Then you know how it will come out."[24]

7

The Presence
and the Power of God

The Christian church came into existence with the benediction, "The grace of the Lord Jesus Christ and the love of God and the fellowship of the Holy Spirit be with you all" (2 Cor. 13:14). It is in the fellowship of the Holy Spirit that we know the grace of the Lord Jesus Christ and the love of God. The Holy Spirit, the presence and the power of God, makes the church a living community and gives personal, existential reality to the believers' faith.

The church is God's gracious gift. The words of the risen Jesus to his disciples are the church's charter: " 'Peace be with you. As the Father has sent me, even so I send you.' And when he had said this, he breathed on them, and said to them, 'Receive the Holy Spirit' " (John 20:21–22). Karl Barth put the same truth more theologically when he declared that the reality and the unity of the church are in the hearing of the Word of God.[1] John Calvin's first reference to predestination is found in his discussion of the church.[2] The church is the elect of God. God creates the church by his Word and by his Spirit. All human activity is a response to the power and the presence of God, and no human program or organization is necessary for the existence of the church. We cannot by working hard bring the church into existence.

The church is composed of those who have received the Spirit. "If you want to be assured that you are really a member of the Church, really incorporated in Christ, look at the manifest presence of the Spirit."[3] The Spirit, not baptism and certainly not confirmation, is the first mark of membership. "Because you are sons, God has sent the Spirit of his Son into our hearts, crying, 'Abba! Father!' " (Gal. 4:6). "By this we know that he abides in us, by the Spirit which he has given us" (1 John 3:24).

The book of Acts reports the final words of the risen Jesus in a way that speaks even more abruptly to contemporary people and to the

organized church today. "He charged them not to depart from Jerusalem, but to wait for the promise of the Father, which, he said, 'you
heard from me, for John baptized with water, but before many days
you shall be baptized with the Holy Spirit' " (Acts 1:4–5). The command of the risen Jesus is to wait, before we organize the church or
plan its mission or appoint a task force to write a position paper, until
we have been baptized with the Holy Spirit.[4]

The promise of the risen Jesus—Receive the Holy Spirit—speaks
on the one hand in rebuke to the matter-of-factness of the organized
church, and on the other hand to a pervasive emptiness, not only in
the life of the church but in the life of our society. For many people,
in the church as in society, God is absent. Our cultural ethos has
become opaque to the divine presence and to the power of God.
Autonomous realms in our common life, education, civic and social
life, science, medical practice, and business operate as if there were
no God, or at least as if there were no need for God. It is assumed
by our culture that God is not necessary. And yet the yearning per-
sists, and in our secular culture, so much of which operates with no
reference to the living God, there has occurred a religious revival
that has persisted for at least four decades, as well as the emergence
of strange forms of religion, from astrology to faith healing. Even in
communist lands, officially dedicated to the eradication of religion,
religion has demonstrated an unusual capacity to survive. For over
a century historians, psychologists, social reformers, and philosophers
have been busy explaining religion away. And yet it does not go
away. The human spirit overwhelmingly reaches out even in inchoate and diffused ways to what the New Testament calls the Holy
Spirit, the power and the presence of the living God. It is instructive
to note that in the past thirty years, the churches that have grown
most rapidly in American life unashamedly bear witness to the promise of the risen Christ: Receive the Holy Spirit.

Who Is the Holy Spirit?

Who is the Holy Spirit? The church knew the reality of the Spirit
long before it could say who the Spirit is. The Holy Spirit is the reality
that impinges upon our lives, that moves us and draws us. In his
presence we are both fascinated and overwhelmed. But the Holy
Spirit is not within our grasp, and not at our disposal. Hence we have
to speak of the Holy Spirit, but we can only speak of the Holy Spirit
as that reality which encounters us but which we cannot objectify.
We are therefore forced to speak in terms of images and analogies.

When the church was finally compelled by internal as well as
external questions to declare what it believed, the church affirmed

that "the Holy Spirit [is] the Lord and giver of life, who proceeds from the Father and the Son; who with the Father and the Son together is worshiped and glorified; who spoke by the prophets." The church was simply and plainly saying that the Spirit is the way or mode of the presence of the risen Christ in the church. As Gregory of Nyssa, whose theology influenced the Council of Constantinople (381), expressed it, the Holy Spirit is a mode or way of God's being God.

No Reformed theologian has so clearly answered the question of who is the Holy Spirit as has Karl Barth:

> The Holy Spirit . . . is God, attesting himself to the spirit of man as his God, as the God who acts for him and to him. He is God, coming to man, and coming to him in such a way that he is revealed to him as the God who reconciles the world and man to himself, in such a way therefore that what he is and does for him as such becomes the Word which man can hear and actually does hear, in such a way, therefore, that man allows himself to be reconciled with him (2 Cor. 5:20). God's self-attestation makes what he does the Word which is spoken to this man and received and accepted by him. The Holy Spirit is God in this his self-attestation—God in the power which quickens man to this profitable and living knowledge of his action. He is God intervening and acting for man, addressing himself to him, in such a way that he says Yes to himself and this makes possible and necessary man's human Yes to him.[5]

John V. Taylor, the Anglican bishop and mission society secretary, in a very remarkable book, *The Go-Between God,* speaks of the Holy Spirit with analogies drawn from our own human experience. The spirit of a person is not so much the power of being alive, but the power by which one is who he or she is, the power by which one makes oneself known to another, the power also to recognize others and to relate to them in a personal way. The Holy Spirit, then, is the power of the divine personhood by which God makes himself known, and grasps and moves the lives of human beings.[6]

The Holy Spirit is God in action in nature and in history. Yet this leaves the Spirit undefined in a world in which there are many false spirits. The Holy Spirit is distinguished from the false spirits by being the Spirit of Jesus Christ. As Karl Barth has put it, "We cannot say more of the Holy Spirit and his work than that he is the power in which Jesus Christ attests himself, attests himself effectively, creating in man response and obedience."[7] John Calvin identifies the Holy Spirit more specifically. The Holy Spirit is indissolubly united to the words of scripture. The Holy Spirit who inspired the words of scripture is bound to that Word.[8]

In sum, the Holy Spirit is God in his divine power and presence at work in nature and history, the God whom we know in Jesus Christ, a revelation attested to us by the inspiration of the Holy Spirit in the words of scripture. The Holy Spirit lays bare our created, finite, historical character. We cannot control the Spirit, though the church has often tried by fastening the Holy Spirit to sacred things, places, or people. But the Holy Spirit is free. We have to wait for the Spirit. The occasions when the Holy Spirit is present to us cannot be predicted, and they cannot be repeated at will. The Christian life and the church itself always have the quality of a gift.

The Holy Spirit and the Christian Witness

The first work of the Holy Spirit, the work on which the whole thesis of this book depends, is to bear witness to Jesus Christ. "When the Counselor comes, whom I shall send to you from the Father, even the Spirit of truth, who proceeds from the Father, he will bear witness to me" (John 15:26). The historical fact of Jesus Christ makes no one a Christian. Neither does the Christian tradition, which is passed on in living memory and in books and creeds. The Spirit bears witness and enables us to know that God encounters us in this man, that Jesus Christ is our savior.

Historians and theologians can never explain why the historical fact of Jesus Christ should have created such a community. Neither can they explain why the memory, scriptures, and symbols of this tradition maintain their power in the lives of Christian people and in Christian communities today. The power is not in the words, written or oral, in the theological speculation, in the sacraments, or in the organization. Albert Outler states: "A doctrinal system, a developed liturgy, a settled polity, all these are achievements possible only within a community that has its life and power from another originating source than these. . . . It is the Spirit who performs the *actus tradendi,* and so makes Christ our contemporary."[9] None of this means that the works of theology, polity, worship, and administration are unimportant. Indeed, the Spirit makes use of them and blesses faithful labor. It does mean that without the Spirit, theology is an academic exercise as limited in its use as the secular polities and rituals of our time.

The presence of the Holy Spirit restores to us the assurance that there is such a thing as the "faith which was once for all delivered [handed over] to the saints" (Jude 3) without its becoming a deadly dull law. No one has understood this better than Outler:

> The origin and center of our faith and our community . . . is God's self-manifestation in Jesus Christ who possesses all men who receive him (John 1:12). It is God's prime act of *tradition*—or "handing over"

Jesus Christ to share our existence and to effect our salvation. "For he who did not spare his own Son but 'handed him over' [*paredōken auton*] for us all, will he not also give us all things else with him?" (Romans 8:31–32; cf. also Romans 4:24–25).

This divine "tradition," or *paradosis,* was a divine act in human history—and it is renewed and made contemporary in the ongoing course of history by the act of God's Holy Spirit, whom Jesus "handed over" to his disciples in the last hour on the cross (*paredōken to pneuma,* John 19:30). The Holy Spirit—"whom the Father will send in my name" (John 14:26)—re-creates the original act of tradition *(traditum)* by an act of "traditioning" *(actus tradendi),* so that the tradition of Jesus Christ becomes a living force in later lives and in faith based on response to a contemporary witness. It is this *actus tradendi* which changes a man's historical knowledge of Jesus Christ—far away and long ago—into vital faith in Jesus Christ—"*my* Lord and *my* God!" . . .

God's *traditum* was received by the Apostles and the Church—by the descent of the Spirit which enabled them to be witnesses to Jesus Christ in Jerusalem and in all Judea and Samaria and to the end of the earth (Acts 1:8; cf. 3:22). This testimony to the total Event of Christ—and its saving import—became the essence of the apostolic preaching. What they had received they felt commissioned to hand on to others.[10]

Our Christian witness is subordinate to the witness of the Spirit. We are called to bring to the Christian witness the greatest human competencies, but it is equally important to know that, without the Spirit who bears witness to Jesus Christ, all is vain. It is the Spirit who enables us to say, "Abba, Father," to know that Jesus is the Christ, who gives life to the symbols, the creeds, the theology of the church. The first work of the Spirit is to bear witness to Jesus Christ.

The Holy Spirit and the Church

The Holy Spirit also works in the human self and in the life of the church. The Holy Spirit is God personally at work in the world. In common discourse, spirit frequently stands in contrast with the material. This is almost never the case with the Holy Spirit. The Holy Spirit is in contrast not to the material but to the impersonal. The Holy Spirit is God personally at work to inspire, to make alive, to convince, to enable Christians to speak and act as Christians, to form the church.

In summarizing the work of the Holy Spirit we can do no better than to follow John Calvin's outline of the work of the Spirit in the third book of the *Institutes of the Christian Religion.*

The Holy Spirit *unites* us with Jesus Christ and his work for us and our salvation. It is not enough to know Jesus Christ as an objective historical fact, to know that Jesus Christ is for us, unless we also know that Jesus Christ is *in* us, not substantially but in a personal union. Reformed theologians would later speak of this union in a federal way: that is, in terms of representation and structure. This did serve to provide an objective structure to the union.

Calvin, however, speaks of our union with Christ in personal terms. The nearest analogy we are likely to find for this union is in the experience we have with other human beings when we are deeply united with them, not simply in some common work but in a personal unity from which we receive power and strength. In a very real sense, one person can live within another person. Not infrequently we say, There goes so-and-so all over again, meaning that the life of one person is so incorporated into the life of another that the other reflects this life. Surely the apostle Paul meant something similar to what we do know in analogous but weaker ways in human experience when he said, "It is no longer I who live, but Christ who lives in me; and the life I now live in the flesh I live by faith in the Son of God, who loved me and gave himself for me" (Gal. 2:20).

The principal work of the Holy Spirit is *faith,* which Calvin describes as confidence and trust in the mercy of God as revealed in Jesus Christ. Faith, as is the case with other human attitudes such as humility, gratitude, and love, is beyond the power of the will. Faith is always elicited by the reality in whom we repose our trust and confidence. Moreover, faith on any level is inhibited by the corruption of our hearts and the density of our minds. Thus Calvin speaks of the Holy Spirit as purifying our hearts and illuminating our minds. On the one hand, the Holy Spirit lays hold of us in such a way as to overcome our self-centeredness, and on the other hand the Holy Spirit inspires us to see what we had not seen before. The Holy Spirit provides new images and arouses our imagination. In addition, the Holy Spirit confirms this new relationship, this new openness and trust, by establishing it in our hearts. We all know something of this in relationships with other people. We know how the spirit of another has encountered our spirit, enabling us to see on the human level what we did not see before, eliciting from us acts of love and courage of which we had previously been incapable, and then confirming this relationship in our lives.

John Calvin also speaks of the Holy Spirit as testifying in our hearts that the words of scripture are verily the words of God. Calvin does not relate the work of *testimony* in the first book of the *Institutes* to the work of *illumination* eliciting faith in the third book. And yet they belong together. The words of scripture can be an objective fact, a selection of Near Eastern literature that can be appreciated simply as literature. Moreover, most of us have had the experience of reading scripture when it is so many words. And then, under the power of the Holy Spirit, these words become to us verily the Word of God. Calvin despaired of any external authority convincing us that scripture is the Word of God. The church cannot do it. Arguments from reason cannot do it. Only the Holy Spirit can testify in our hearts as we read the words of scripture that these are the words of God. In this sense the authority of scripture is self-authenticating under the power of the Holy Spirit. The work of the Holy Spirit in illuminating our hearts and minds and in testifying to our hearts that scripture is the Word of God is not arbitrary and certainly not in contradiction to human reason. The conviction that the Bible is the Word of God is rational and credible, but it is not a conclusion of reason. It is first of all an experience of faith elicited by the Holy Spirit, which in life seeks intelligibility.

The Holy Spirit who unites us to Christ and works faith in our hearts also regenerates us and sanctifies us. *Sanctification* is not a word that is common in contemporary Reformed theology. Yet Reformed theology in the beginning was characterized by its emphasis upon sanctification, while at the same time maintaining that justification by grace through faith was the principal ground upon which the Christian life was established. While the Calvinists insisted that the chief end of man is to glorify God, they always insisted on the human level that this glorification took place in the sanctification of the human life under the power of the Holy Spirit.

Sanctification easily turned into a works righteousness and into a burden. But as Calvin understood it, it was a gift of God's grace. It was an answer to the human question: Can a human life be transformed? Can a misdirected life be turned around? Can human life grow on the one hand in trust for God and on the other in humaneness and readiness to forgive? In the *Institutes of the Christian Religion,* sanctification is a gospel. It is the joyous hope that by the power of the Holy Spirit human life can be turned around and the human self can be sanctified.

The work of the Holy Spirit is above all the *church,* which is the fellowship of the Holy Spirit. The church is not an aggregation of individuals but a community with a common life in the Spirit. Christian existence even more than human existence can be realized only in community. The Holy Spirit makes the common life—that is, life in a common faith—a common style of living and a common hope, a living reality.

Receiving the Holy Spirit

How can we receive the Holy Spirit? In the New Testament, the early Christians were either commanded to receive the Holy Spirit or to wait until the Holy Spirit came. No one in the Christian tradition has understood this any better than the Calvinists, who have always acknowledged the Lordship of God. The Holy Spirit is free, and the Holy Spirit acts according to his own choosing.

For this reason, John Calvin was always skeptical of methods and exercises of the Christian life.[11] It is doubtful if he would be very pleased with the contemporary emphasis upon spiritual formation. It is worth noting that spiritual formation is not a classical Protestant term, much less a Calvinist word. Furthermore, the Calvinists never spoke about spirituality; they always spoke about piety. The exercises they used were always minimal, simple, open, and, they believed, appointed by the New Testament.

The Calvinists from the beginning, however, took seriously the promise of the presence of the Holy Spirit: "Where two or three are gathered in my name, there am I in the midst of them" (Matt. 18:20). In the presence of the inscrutable mystery of the divine freedom, Christians can in hope exercise the promise.

The later tradition would speak of the means of grace, a phrase Calvin does not use. Yet so long as it is understood that the Holy Spirit is not bound to any means, it is appropriate to honor the promise. In the context of these means, God promises to make his presence known.

God's presence is always a mediated presence. Our knowledge of God is through that which is not God. No person has ever seen God and lived. We "know God through the world, or through a person such as Jesus, or through the Bible, or through the necessary truths of reason, or through history."[12] The mediation of God's presence through that which is not God is an accommodation to our created condition. There is an analogy between the mediation of the divine presence and the mediation of the presence of a human self. None of us has ever seen a self. The presence of the self we know and even love is always mediated to us through that which is not the self; namely, the voice, the facial expression, the language of the body. On the human level, the presence of a person is no less real for having been mediated.

The great danger is that the medium of the divine presence will be confused with the reality of God. In confusing God with the medium of revelation we get control of God. If God can somehow be tied to that which is not God but a part of created existence, then we can manage God and even dispense divine grace as though it were a medicine. But the Holy Spirit is not bound to any medium, not even to the Bible or to the sacraments.

The world is God's creation, and hence it is possible to speak of the sacramental universe. Every created thing is an outward and visible sign of the inward and spiritual grace of the Creator. In the Christian community the appointed means of grace are those which have their origin in the work of Jesus Christ and which are attested within the New Testament canon.[13] They communicate to us the specific character of the redemption purchased by Jesus Christ.

The preeminent means of the Spirit's presence is the holy scriptures. Hence the reading of scripture is fundamental to Reformed piety. Protestants have always been distinguished by their emphasis on learning to read. In a day when learning to read becomes part of the cult of modernity, and in particular part of the propaganda of the communist movement, it is important to note that the Protestants taught people to read not so they could read instructions or directions, but so they could read the holy scriptures. This made the individual believer who read the holy scriptures the equal of archbishops and kings.[14] The social and political consequences were immense. The primary purpose, however, was to read holy scripture so that through the words of scripture the eternal God would speak to the human heart.

Calvin in his discussion of the Christian life devotes an entire chapter to prayer, which he believed was the principal exercise of faith and a primary means of God's grace. He advocated and prepared prayers for five to nine occasions in daily life, depending on how many meals one ate. The Christian was to pray on waking up, on sitting down to a meal, on finishing a meal, on going to work or to school, and on retiring at the end of the day. In traditional Reformed piety, the reading of the Bible and prayer became the principal means in personal life by which the Holy Spirit became alive to human beings.

The Christian life always takes place in the church, and it is as a member of the body of Christ that the Christian reads the Bible and prays. Yet the primary exercise of the church is the gathering of the Christian community to worship God on the Lord's day. Karl Barth is truly a Calvinist when he declares, "Assembling for divine worship is self-evidently the centre and presupposition of the whole Christian life, the atmosphere in which it is lived."[15] In Reformed worship, the center and heart is the proclamation of the Word of God in the sermon and in the sacraments in the hearing and presence of the people. Calvin envisioned a service in which the Word would be preached and the sacraments would be administered, yet it must not be forgotten that the proclamation of the Word has even in Calvin a certain priority over the sacraments. For Calvin the sacraments are appendages that confirm this preaching of the Word. Hence the Westminster Catechisms are not contrary to Calvin when they insist that the reading of the Word of God, but in particular the preaching of the Word of God, is the means by which God's presence and power become alive in our hearts.

This emphasis upon preaching as the means of grace places a very heavy burden upon the minister. The Holy Spirit is not tied to the words of preaching, and neither is the Holy Spirit dependent upon the competence of the preacher. It no doubt has happened on many occasions that the Holy Spirit has made the words of an inept sermon the occasion of the gracious presence of God when the words of a beautiful and brilliant sermon have been left dead and ineffective. Yet it is through the words of the sermon, at least for the Reformed tradition, that God's grace is preeminently conveyed to the Christian community. This lays a great burden on the preacher, on the one hand not to offer unto God that which costs him or her nothing, and on the other hand not to offer unto God words that are inappropriate to God's grace. Hence the tradition has always insisted that preaching must be an explication and application of the grace of God in scripture.

The sacraments for Calvin likewise were important means of the Spirit's presence. He saw baptism as a sign of God's grace that forgives our sins, welcomes us into the household of faith, and engages us to the Lord; and he saw the Lord's Supper as preeminently the sign of the atoning work of Jesus Christ, of our fellowship with one another in the Christian community, and likewise as a testimony of our loyalty to the Lord. The Holy Spirit makes Jesus Christ personally present to us in the sacrament.

Here we must return to the theme with which we began. Calvin understood the Reformation as the evangelization of the church. By this he meant that the government of the church, the preaching of the church, and the sacraments must be so freed of human inventions that through the simplicity of the church fellowship, of preaching, and of the sacraments God's grace could speak. Nothing is so characteristic of Calvin as his effort to rid the life of the church—and, in particular, preaching and the sacraments—from the "theatrical trifles" by which human beings attempt to enhance the psychological impact of either. Calvinist preaching has always been *plain-style* preaching, and the Calvinist sacraments have likewise been free of human inventions.

The attempt to "enrich" worship and the sacraments, in particular with psychological nostrums designed to elicit a human response, may be a sign of unbelief. The addition of what Calvin labeled "theatrical trifles" may stand in the way of God's grace.

In the whole history of Christian thought, no one has known better than the Calvinists that our salvation is finally rooted in the election of God and that God's Spirit speaks anywhere he chooses. Yet it is *not* out of keeping with that tradition to emphasize, as later Calvinists sometimes did, that there is more likelihood that God shall speak to us if we place ourselves within the fellowship of the Christian community and under the means of grace which the Holy Spirit appointed in the New Testament. Here we can wait for the presence and the power of God, but we can wait with the promise that where two or three are gathered together in his name, there God shall be graciously present.

The characteristically Reformed gospel for this day is, Receive the Holy Spirit. It is the optimism that the power and the presence of God will become real in our lives not when we undertake elaborate exercises and procedures, many of which are obviously autosuggestive, but when we place ourselves in the presence of the very simple means of the divine grace in scripture, in the sacraments, in prayer, in the fellowship of the Christian community. The Holy Spirit is not in our control. The Holy Spirit speaks when and where he chooses. Yet there is the promise that the Holy Spirit is present in the midst of those who gather to worship and hear the Word of God, and that God makes himself known to us through the means which he has appointed.

Epilogue

The church in an increasingly secular and pagan society must be strong and clear in proclaiming its essential message. Much of what has been written in this book belonged also to culture a generation ago. The organized church could survive even if it neglected its unique message. The great need was relevance, being on the cutting edge. The faith and life of the church could be taken for granted. The message and the symbols of the faith were alive in the social structures and memory. This is less and less the situation in which we live. If four decades ago we had the message without relevance, today we are in danger of being relevant without a message.

The substance of this book can be put very plainly and succinctly in biblical texts.

Chapter 1: "But how are men to call upon him in whom they have not believed? And how are they to believe in him of whom they have never heard? And how are they to hear without a preacher? . . . 'How beautiful are the feet of those who preach good news!' " (Rom. 10:14–15).

Chapter 2: "And the Word became flesh and dwelt among us, full of grace and truth; we have beheld his glory, glory as of the only Son from the Father" (John 1:15).

Chapter 3: "For I am not ashamed of the gospel: it is the power of God for salvation to every one who has faith, to the Jew first and also to the Greek" (Rom. 1:16).

Chapter 4: "We know that in everything God works for good with those who love him, who are called according to his purpose" (Rom. 8:28).

Chapter 5: "He chose us in him before the foundation of the world, that we should be holy and blameless before him. He destined us in love to be his sons through Jesus Christ, according to the purpose of his will, to the praise of his glorious grace which he freely bestowed on us in the Beloved" (Eph. 1:4–6).

Chapter 6: "Then I saw a new heaven and a new earth; for the first heaven and the first earth had passed away, and the sea was no more. And I saw the holy city, new Jerusalem, coming down out of heaven from God, prepared as a bride adorned for her husband; and I heard a loud voice from the throne saying, 'Behold, the dwelling of God is with men. He will dwell with them, and they shall be his people, and God himself will be with them; he will wipe away every tear from their eyes, and death shall be no more, neither shall there be mourning nor crying nor pain any more, for the former things have passed away'" (Rev. 21:1–4).

Chapter 7: "Jesus said to them again, 'Peace be with you. As the Father has sent me, even so I send you.' And when he had said this, he breathed on them, and said to them, 'Receive the Holy Spirit'" (John 20: 21–22).

We live on the one hand in the church in which these texts are very familiar, so that we sometimes forget how momentous they are. On the other hand, we live in a culture that is indifferent to Christian faith in particular and to religion in general. Our old familiarity with these texts and the indifference of our culture alike rob us of the enthusiasm of proclaiming the greatest good news that ever came to human beings on this planet.

These texts are somewhat arbitrarily chosen. They are, however, a fair summary of the church's unique message, of what the church has to say that no one else can say, and of the message for which human hearts, in spite of the attractions and distractions of our culture, desperately need to hear. The proper response to these texts is in the great hymns of the faith such as "All People That on Earth Do Dwell," "A Mighty Fortress Is Our God," "How Firm a Foundation," and "Now Thank We All Our God." These texts and hymns are sufficient to enable ordinary people to live with grace, serenity, and dignity amid the joys and sorrows, the successes and defeats of life.

This faith is our heritage and trust. It is our heritage because it has been given to us not only by the grace of God but also by the Christian community. Between us and the original disciples there is an unbroken succession of witnesses. Every Christian has come to the faith by the testimony of a witness. For many this heritage has been bequeathed by birth in the Christian family and in the fellowship of the Christian church. The faith has also been transmitted through culture. Through the centuries Christianity became a part of the literature, the institutions, and the rituals of society. Until very recently anyone born in a Western culture grew up bearing the marks of the faith. Conversion was sometimes little more than movement into the organized life of the church, and at other times it was the intensification of what was already implicitly believed.

Today the situation is increasingly different. The pluralism of our society has made it more and more necessary for each person to choose his or her faith. The mobility of society and the dominance of the mass media have made it less and less possible for communities of faith to protect the faith of the old, much less the young. Hence any community of faith that endures in this society must learn to witness to the faith and to nurture the faith. The preaching, teaching, and nurturing of the church must be much stronger in the new society than in the old order in which society itself supported the Christian way. The Christian today must know what he or she believes and be able to state that faith in simple sentences which illuminate human experience.

The Christian witness must be confessional. This simply means that we tell people what this faith has meant to us and we invite them to share it. As God in Christ asks for our free response, so we must honor the freedom of those to whom we witness. Therefore we dare not attempt to coerce faith.

We cannot prove a faith. Every faith is rooted in some human experience which has become a window to what is truly real or to what is the clue that unlocks the meaning of human life. Every human being lives by faith. There is no other possibility. We cannot get outside of human life or of the world. We all live within the brackets and we have to live in the light of clues or "revelations" of what is outside the brackets. Christians are distinguished not by the fact that they live by faith, but by the fact that they live by faith in Jesus Christ. The Christian confession is that Jesus Christ has brought us salvation.

The fact that we all live by faith does not mean even in a pluralistic society that one faith is as good as another. As there is a difference between faith and credulity, so there is a difference between a faith that is adequate for life and a faith that is destructive to life. In chapter 1 the ways faith validates itself were outlined. In witnessing we can only confess: that is, tell others what this faith is and what it has done for us. Our witness must always honor the integrity of the human mind and the freedom of the self.

Confession has to be done in humility for at least three reasons. First, that which we confess is a gift, a gift from God and a gift from others. Second, our apprehension of the God whom we confess is broken and limited by our time, space, personhood, and intelligence as well as by our sin. Finally, we do not confess what *we* have done, but what God has done for us and all people.

Our limited and broken apprehension of God's grace does not mean that God is limited. The stupendous claim is that the Christian witness points to God, who has created the world and now rules, judges, and redeems the creation. The bearing of this witness is the highest dignity and the greatest service a human being can render to other human beings on this planet.

The exact form the Christian witness will take in the next decades in American society is not clear. Many in the church welcomed the secularization of society and the development of a pluralism of religions and life-styles as wholesome for the life of faith. Paul Tillich was surely correct in saying that Protestantism is healthiest when it is subjected to criticism from without. Yet an increasingly secular and pluralistic society presents problems for the transmission of faith that the church has not yet concretely faced. New questions must be answered in the very near future. Is it possible to transmit a faith in a society where education is secular on both the elementary and university levels? Can the church transmit the faith without schools which in some sense teach the faith and support it or at least teach in such a way that Christian faith is an open option? A second question has to do with the mass media. How do you transmit the faith in a culture that is exposed to mass media that continually proclaim alien faiths but are seldom instruments for Christian proclamation? A third question has to do with the transmission of the faith in a culture in which the social settings of life do not undergird and support either Christian faith or a Christian manner of living. Finally, it is becoming increasingly clear that a highly pluralistic society does not have sufficient consensus in the basic understanding of the meaning of human existence and of the world to have any satisfactory resolution of problems such as abortion, the death penalty, various issues that arise out of human sexuality, and the morality of a welfare state. How can the church give a prophetic witness to society when there are no common faith commitments in the society or when the official witness of the church does not grow out of the community of faith or receive support from the community of faith?

This book has been written in the conviction that no matter how the church resolves the problems of a Christian witness in a secular society, there is not now nor will there be a substitute for the Christian witness in preaching, teaching, and pastoral care in the life of the church itself. The enhancement of pastoral care as well as preaching and teaching will continue to be the human means by which the church lives in a society that gives no support to being Christian. The recovery of the integrity and competence of preaching, teaching, and pastoral care in the tradition of the Reformed, Protestant, and

Christian faith is the precondition for the Christian community's meeting the challenge of a secular and perhaps an increasingly pagan culture.

The crisis in the church today is aggravated by the refusal of many people, some prominent in culture and some prominent in the leadership of the church, to take theological issues seriously, to understand that the great human problem is not social, political, economic, psychological, or physical but theological.

Time magazine reported in its issue of May 24, 1954, the result of a poll of twenty-eight prominent Americans who were asked to rate the hundred most important single events in world history. First place was given to Columbus's discovery of America, and second place went to Gutenberg's movable type. Jesus' crucifixion was preceded by thirteen other events.

One may argue on the basis of verifiable consequences that Jesus Christ changed history more than any other event, though this judgment is debatable.

If Jesus Christ, however, is who we as Christian people say he is, the Word become flesh, then no other event in human history can compare with his birth, life, death, and resurrection. Someone may say the Christian affirmation is not true. But if it is true, no one can say it is unimportant. It is the greatest good news that ever came to human beings on this planet. No other work can possibly compare with the significance of proclaiming this gospel to all people everywhere.

Notes

Preface

1. Based on Minutes of the General Assembly of the Presbyterian Church (U.S.A.).

2. *Emerging Trends,* published by the Princeton Religion Research Center, March 1983.

3. *Religion in America, The Gallup Report No. 222,* March 1984.

4. *Forbes,* December 1, 1986, pp. 220–221.

5. A. James Reichley, *Religion in American Public Life* (Washington, D.C.: The Brookings Institution, 1985), pp. 273, 275; *Emerging Trends,* May 1984, p. 6.

Chapter 1: Christian Witness Today

1. Thesis 62. Theodore Tappert, ed., *Selected Writings of Martin Luther, 1517–1520* (Philadelphia: Fortress Press, 1967), p. 57.

2. John H. Leith, ed., *Creeds of the Churches,* 3rd ed. (Atlanta: John Knox Press, 1982), p. 129.

3. Cf. W. A. Visser 't Hooft, "Evangelism Among Europe's Neo-Pagans," *International Review of Mission,* vol. 66, no. 264 (October 1977), pp. 349ff.

4. Insight gained from personal conversation with Professor Albert C. Outler. In a recent study, Ronald Thiemann has written: "For modern thinkers, communal acceptance must always follow philosophical demonstration. A faith which assumes the truth of its background beliefs and seeks simply to understand them cannot flourish in an atmosphere which demands justification prior to belief. Under these changed modern circumstances faith seeking understanding inevitably becomes faith seeking foundation." *Revelation and Theology: The Gospel as Narrated Promise* (Notre Dame: University of Notre Dame Press, 1985), p. 14.

See also Clifford Geertz, an anthropologist, in an essay "Religion as a Cultural System": "It seems to me that it is best to begin any approach to this issue [the meaning of belief] with frank recognition that religious belief involves not a Baconian induction from everyday experience—for then we should all be agnostics—but rather a prior acceptance of faith which transforms that experience. . . . The basic axiom underlying what we may call 'The religious perspective' is everywhere the same: He who would know must first believe." *The Interpretation of Cultures: Selected Essays* (New York: Basic Books, 1973), pp. 109–110.

5. Lewis W. Spitz, *The Protestant Reformation 1511–1559* (New York: Harper & Row, 1985), p. 4; see also John Calvin, "The Necessity of Reforming the Church," in *Calvin: Theological Treatises*, ed. by J. K. S. Reid, Library of Christian Classics (Philadelphia: Westminster Press, 1954), pp. 184–216.

6. Lucien Febvre, *A New Kind of History*, ed. by Peter Burke, tr. by K. Folca (New York: Harper & Row, 1973), p. 88.

7. A. G. Dickens and John Tonkin, *The Reformation in Historical Thought* (Cambridge: Harvard University Press, 1985), pp. 234ff.

8. Arthur C. Cochrane, ed., *Reformed Confessions of the Sixteenth Century* (Philadelphia: Westminster Press, 1966), pp. 55–56.

9. Leith, p. 133.

10. Shorter Catechism, Question 89. Philip Schaff, ed., *The Creeds of Christendom*, vol. 3 (New York: Harper & Brothers, 1877), pp. 695–696.

11. Cf. Sydney Ahlstrom, *A Religious History of the American People* (New Haven, Conn.: Yale University Press, 1972), chs. 8–10, 17–20.

12. Herbert Butterfield, *Christianity and History* (London: G. Bell & Sons, 1954), p. 131.

13. See Calvin's preface to his *Commentary on Romans* and the Westminster Directory for Worship.

14. Reinhold Niebuhr, *Leaves from the Notebook of a Tamed Cynic* (Cleveland: World Publishing Co., 1929), p. 27.

15. "There are eloquent passages in Calvin's sermons, but, fearful, perhaps of losing control over himself, and relying on Scripture as a bridle, he composed few eloquent sermons" ("Calvinism as *Theologia Rhetorica*," by William J. Bouwsma, a chapter in his *John Calvin: A Sixteenth-Century Portrait* [New York: Oxford University Press, 1987]).

16. Albert C. Outler, ed., *The Works of John Wesley*, vol. 1: *Sermons I* (Nashville: Abingdon Press, 1984), p. 16.

17. "The distinctive quality of Reformed worship was as much influenced by the character of the congregation as by the literary or musical vehicles of its praise. . . . To assess the Reformed services truly, one must consider the teaching, discipline, witness, and work of the congregation in relation to the worship" (James Hastings Nichols, *Corporate Worship in the Reformed Tradition* [Philadelphia: Westminster Press, 1968], p. 51).

18. Outler, pp. 13, 16–17.

19. Nichols, p. 32.

20. "Lectures on the Epistle to the Hebrews 1517–1518," in *Luther: Early Theological Works*, tr. and ed. by James Atkinson, LCC (Philadelphia: Westminster Press, 1962), pp. 194–195.

21. Karl Barth, *Church Dogmatics*, vol. IV/1 (Edinburgh: T. & T. Clark, 1956), pp. 650ff.

22. Leith, pp. 61ff.

23. Calvin, Commentary on Isaiah 55:11.

24. Calvin, Commentary on 2 Corinthians 2:15; Isaiah 6:10.

25. "If there be one day in the week reserved for religious instruction when they have spent six days in their own business, they are apt to spend the day which is set apart for worship, in play and pastime; some rove about the fields, others go to taverns to quaff; and there are undoubtedly at this time as many at the last mentioned place, as we are assembled here in the name of God" (Calvin, Sermon on 1 Timothy 3:16). See Rodolphe Peter, "Genève dans la prédication de Calvin," in *Calvinus Ecclesiae Genevensis Custos*, ed. by Wilhelm Niesel (Frankfurt am Main: Verlag Peter Lang, 1984), pp. 23–47.

26. Origen, "Exhortation to Martyrdom," in *Alexandrian Christianity*, ed. by Henry Chadwick and J. E. L. Oulton, LCC (Philadelphia: Westminster Press, 1954), p. 396.

27. Carlos M. N. Eire, *War Against the Idols: The Reformation of Worship from Erasmus to Calvin* (Cambridge: Cambridge University Press, 1986), ch. 7.

28. Barth, *Church Dogmatics* vol. I/1, pp. 26–44, 36, 198–227.

29. On historical facts see Emil Brunner, *The Christian Doctrine of Creation and Redemption* (Philadelphia: Westminster Press, 1952), pp. 239ff.; on the work of the Holy Spirit, see Albert C. Outler, *The Christian Tradition and the Unity We Seek* (New York: Oxford University Press, 1957), p. 111.

30. Reinhold Niebuhr, *Faith and History* (New York: Charles Scribner's Sons, 1949), esp. ch. X, "The Validation of the Christian View of Life and History"; John C. Bennett, "Are There Tests of Revelation?" in Donald Walhout, *Interpreting Religion* (Englewood Cliffs, N.J.: Prentice-Hall, 1963), pp. 56–66; Alan Richardson, *Christian Apologetics* (New York: Harper & Brothers, 1947); David Tracy, *Blessed Rage for Order* (New York: Seabury Press, 1975); Schubert Ogden, *On Theology* (San Francisco: Harper & Row, 1986), esp. ch. 1, "What Is Theology?" The debate precipitated by George Lindbeck's *The Nature of Doctrine* (Philadelphia: Westminster Press, 1984) also focuses attention on both the integrity and truth of Christian doctrine. William Placher has written an excellent analysis of this debate, entitled "Postliberal Theology," which is soon to be published in *The Modern Theologians*, edited by David Ford. For an excellent analysis of issues raised here, see Ronald F. Thiemann, *Revelation and Theology: The Gospel as Narrated Promise* (Notre Dame, Ind.: University of Notre Dame Press, 1987).

31. H. Richard Niebuhr, *The Meaning of Revelation* (New York: Macmillan Co., 1941), p. 52.

32. The Enlightenment refers to the dominant intellectual movement of the eighteenth century: deism in England, illuminism in France, and the Enlightenment in Germany. It was a revolt against traditional authorities and placed emphasis upon reason as the basis for deciding issues. The Enlightenment emphasized that reason and education can bring about a better future. Kant answered the question, What is the Enlightenment? by exclaiming, "Enlightenment is man's release from his self-incurred tutelage. Tute-

lage is man's inability to make use of his understanding without direction from another. . . . Dare to know! Have courage to use your own reason!—that is the motto of the Enlightenment" (Immanuel Kant, *What Is Enlightenment?* tr. and ed. by L. W. Beck [bound with *Foundations of the Metaphysics of Morals;* Indianapolis: Bobbs-Merrill Co., 1959], p. 286).

In this discussion the Enlightenment and the nineteenth century stand for a complex of ideas, some in conflict with each other, but all of which required a response from the Christian community in its understanding of its faith. (1) The calling into question of all external authorities and the use of doubt as a means of arriving at truth. A new morality of knowledge making each person responsible for truth. (2) A positive attitude toward change as the normal condition of life. (3) The scientific revolution, especially issues raised for theology by Copernicus and Darwin. (4) The scientific study of religion (history, psychology, sociology). (5) Karl Marx. (6) Sigmund Freud. (7) Nietzsche. (8) The industrial revolution. (9) A new social context, pluralistic and dominated by mass media.

For discussion of these challenges to Christian faith and community, see the following: Langdon Gilkey, *Naming the Whirlwind: The Renewal of God-Language* (Indianapolis: Bobbs-Merrill Co., 1969), and *Reaping the Whirlwind: A Christian Interpretation of History* (New York: Seabury Press, 1976); Karl Barth, *Protestant Theology in the Nineteenth Century: Its Background and History* (Valley Forge: Judson Press, 1973); Claude Welch, *Protestant Theology in the Nineteenth Century,* vols. 1, 2 (New Haven: Yale University Press, 1972, 1985).

33. Northrup Frye, *The Educated Imagination* (Bloomington, Ind.: Indiana University Press, 1964), p. 110.

34. Karl Barth, "Foreword," in Heinrich Heppe, *Reformed Dogmatics,* tr. by G. T. Thomson (1950; Grand Rapids: Baker Publishing House, 1978), pp. v–vii; Paul Tillich, *A History of Christian Thought* (New York: Simon & Schuster, 1967), pp. 276–283.

35. Critical orthodoxy was called to public attention by *Essays Catholic and Critical,* ed. by Edward Gordon Selwyn (London: SPCK, 1926), written by Anglicans who wished to be Christian and also to do justice to modern knowledge. "For the two terms Catholic and critical represent principles, habits, and tempers of the religious mind which only reach their maturity in combination. To the first belongs everything in us that acknowledges and adores the one abiding, transcendent, and supremely given Reality, God; believes in Jesus Christ, as the unique revelation in true personal form of His mystery; and recognizes His Spirit embodied in the Church as the authoritative and ever-living witness of His will, word, and work. To the second belongs the exercise of that divinely implanted gift of reason by which we measure, sift, examine, and judge whatever is proposed for our belief, whether it be a theological doctrine or a statement of historical fact, and so establish, deepen, and purify our understanding of the truth of the Gospel. The proportion in which these two activities are blended will vary in different individuals and in relation to different parts of our subject-matter: but there is no point at which they do not interact, and we are convinced that this interaction is necessary to any present-

ment of Christianity which is to claim the allegiance of the world today" (p. vi).

In these lectures orthodoxy is defined more in terms of the Bible and classical Protestantism. Orthodoxy, while defying precise definition, is more easily defined than modern knowledge. Modern knowledge and the "assured results" of research have often proved time-bound and fragile. For example, the closed picture of the world and the self as a function of the brain no longer square with the judgment of many of the ablest scientists. Christians ought to be at least as critical of the orthodoxies of science and culture as they are of the orthodoxies of theology. See Claude Welch, *Protestant Theology in the Nineteenth Century*, vol. 1, chs. 10 and 11.

36. *Early Christian Fathers*, ed. by Cyril C. Richardson, LCC (Philadelphia: Westminster Press, 1953), p. 272.

37. James Turner, *Without God, Without Creed* (Baltimore: Johns Hopkins University Press, 1985), pp. 266–269.

38. E.g., Herbert Butterfield, *The Origins of History* (New York: Basic Books, 1981), pp. 162–168.

39. Barth, *Church Dogmatics*, vol. IV/1, p. 646; vol. IV/3, pp. 109ff. See ch. 7, "The Presence and the Power of God," for a discussion of the work of the Holy Spirit, who "re-creates the original act of tradition by an act of traditioning, so that the tradition of Jesus Christ becomes a living force in later lives and in faith based on response to a contemporary witness" (Outler, *The Christian Tradition and the Unity We Seek*, note 29).

40. Reinhold Niebuhr, *The Nature and Destiny of Man* (New York: Charles Scribner's Sons, 1943), vol. 1, pp. 123–149; vol. 2, pp. 6, 52–53, 63–64, 69.

41. See Stephen Sykes, *The Identity of Christianity* (Philadelphia: Fortress Press, 1984). Brief summaries of the faith abound: Irenaeus, *Proof of the Apostolic Preaching;* Augustine, *Enchiridion;* Luther's Catechisms; Calvin's Catechisms; Karl Barth, *Dogmatics in Outline* (New York: Philosophical Library, 1949).

42. Karl Rahner, *Theological Investigations* (New York: Crossroad Publishing Co., 1982), vol. 1, p. 69.

Chapter 2: Mystery and Revelation

1. Ignatius, Letter to the Magnesians, par. 8, in *Early Christian Fathers*, ed. by Cyril C. Richardson, LCC (Philadelphia: Westminster Press, 1953), p. 96.

2. Robert Jastrow, *Until the Sun Dies* (New York: W. W. Norton & Co., 1977), ch. 1. See Jastrow's address at Yale Divinity School, "Science and the Creation," in *Reflection*, 1980. Also "Have Astronomers Found God?" *New York Times Magazine*, June 15, 1978; James S. Trefil, *The Moment of Creation* (New York: Charles Scribner's Sons, 1983).

3. Richard E. Leakey and Roger Lewin, *Origins: What New Discoveries Reveal About the Emergence of Our Species and Its Possible Future* (New York: E. P. Dutton, 1977), p. 84.

4. Gabriel Marcel, *Being and Having.* tr. by Katharine Farrer (New York: Harper & Row, 1965), pp. 117–118; Reinhold Niebuhr, *Discerning the Signs of the Times: Sermons for Today and Tomorrow* (New York: Charles Scribner's Sons, 1946), pp. 152–173; Karl Rahner, *Foundations of Christian Faith: An Introduction to the Idea of Christianity,* tr. by William V. Dych (New York: Seabury Press, 1978), pp. 57ff.; Karl Barth, *Church Dogmatics,* vol. III/2 (Edinburgh: T. & T. Clark, 1956), pp. 71–132; Peter Berger, *A Rumor of Angels: Modern Society and the Rediscovery of the Supernatural* (Garden City, N.Y.: Doubleday & Co., 1977).

5. See provocative discussion by Alvin Plantinga: "The Reformed Objection to Natural Theology," in *Christian Scholar's Review,* vol. 10 (1982), pp. 187–198.

6. Marcel, p. 117.

7. Milton Karl Munitz, *The Mystery of Existence* (New York: Appleton-Century-Crofts, 1965), pp. 11–12.

8. Theodore Dobzhansky, *The Biology of Ultimate Concern* (New York: New American Library, 1967), pp. 4–5.

9. Paul Tillich, *A History of Christian Thought: From Its Judaic and Hellenistic Origins to Existentialism,* ed. by Carl E. Braaten (New York: Simon & Schuster, 1968), pp. 71–72. Cf. Roger Williams, *Arius, Heresy and Tradition* (London: Darton, Longman & Todd, 1987), pp. 238ff.; Donald Baillie, *God Was in Christ* (New York: Charles Scribner's Sons, 1948), ch. 3.

10. Cf. George Huntston Williams, "Christology and Church-State Relations in the Fourth Century," *Church History,* vol. 20, no. 3, pp. 3–33; no. 4, pp. 3–25.

11. Albert C. Outler, in an excellent series of lectures as yet unpublished, has summarized what Chalcedon was saying. "The episcopal committee that drafted this definition were not great theologians, but at least they knew what they were trying to do. They took the term *ousia,* that goes back to Origen, as referring to God's mysterious reality; then they took the word *hypostasis* as the word for the mystery as self-revealed, which is mystery having a name in the eyes of faith in response to the light of revelation; they then took the term *prosōpon* from the Antiochene vocabulary as a somewhat awkward synonym for *hypostasis,* but distinguished from *hypostasis* by its stress upon the personification of the self-presentation to the Triune God. The real apple of discord was the term *physis.* To change or to mix the metaphor, this was the bone in the Alexandrine throat. But the Chalcedonian bishops took it, as the Antiochenes had before them and as Maximus the Confessor would two centuries later, to mean 'energy' rather than 'entity,' 'process' rather than 'produce,' 'agency' rather than 'agent.' As well as any modern existentialist they wanted to avoid the claim of objectivizing knowledge, and so they chose the verb *gnōrizomenon* to make this plain. Finally they were determined to spike the batteries on the extreme flanks of the battlefields, and this they did with the four famous adverbs.

"The resulting definition said, in effect, that the best or the best balanced explanation of the mystery of Christ begins with the recognition that the hypostasis of this mystery shares the *ousia* of man, that this hypo-

stasis is a personification of God, that the energy systems of the pro-
claimer and the proclaimee exist in an integral agent and must not be
confused or disjoined. The plain implication of such an explanation as
this is that any further explanation is legitimate and orthodox if it stays
inside these limits, and, conversely, anything beyond these limits runs
out into barren wastes of heresy. And here you have the shaping of the
dogma which is not a settlement of the question, but a definition of the
playing field in which Christological reflection can go on." (From a tape
recording of lectures given at Emory University, 1963. Used by permission.)

12. Arthur C. McGill, *Suffering, A Test of Theological Method*
(Philadelphia: Westminster Press, 1982), p. 66. A splendid account of the
working out of the doctrine of the Trinity may be found in G. L. Prestige,
God in Patristic Thought (London: SPCK, 1952). Prestige concludes (pp.
300–301) with this astute observation: "This orthodox insistence was based
primarily on scriptural fact, but also, as comes out more and more clearly,
on the philosophic sense that the being of God needs to be justified to reason
alike as transcendent, as creative, and as immanent. On the whole these
three adjectives fairly express the special characteristics of the three Persons, at any rate in relation to the universe, which is as far as human knowledge can very well expect to reach. The conception of the Father as
anarchos archē, Source without other source than itself, safeguards the
supremacy of God over created objects and His absolute distinction from
them all. Whatever there was of religious value in the Gnostic assertion
of a divine transcendence so complete that it could not bear direct contact with the world, is preserved when the divine agency in creation is
assigned to God the Son; at the same time, because the Son is fully God,
the truth is maintained that both creation and redemption (or re-crea-
tion) are acts of God. The immanence of the Spirit, in the special work
of sanctification but also in the general guidance of the universe to the end
designed for it, asserts the principle that God is not only transcendent in
the fullest degree, not only active in controlling the world *ab extra*, but
also operative in it from within. It was assumed that the divine relationships
disclosed in the course of revelation, made through religious history and
assisted by reflection on the constitution of the universe, correspond to
real and permanent facts in the life of God. God is self-consistent. In revealing himself to men He cannot be untrue to Himself, or misrepresent His own
nature."

13. Jürgen Moltmann, *The Crucified God: The Cross of Christ as the Foundation and Criticism of Christian Theology*, tr. by R. A. Wilson and John
Bowden (London: SCM Press, 1974), ch. 6.

14. "The organic unity of love, of purpose, of understanding, and of power
disclosed in the one who bears the office of the Christ suggests that selfhood
and personality are the most appropriate terms with which to characterize
God from the Christian standpoint" (John E. Smith, *Experience and God*
[New York: Oxford University Press, 1968], p. 93). "The conviction that God
is personal, and deals personally with men and women, lies at the heart of
Christian experience and thought" (H. H. Farmer, *The World and God: A*

Study of Prayer, Providence, and Miracle in Christian Experience [London: Nisbet & Co., 1942], p. 1).

Chapter 3: The Power of God Unto Salvation

1. W. H. Auden, *For the Time Being* (London: Faber & Faber, 1945), p. 116.

2. Roland Bainton, *Here I Stand: A Life of Martin Luther* (Nashville: Abingdon-Cokesbury Press, 1950), esp. ch. 3.

3. Augustine, *Confessions* 1.1, in *Augustine: Confessions and Enchiridion,* tr. and ed. by Albert C. Outler, LCC (Philadelphia: Westminster Press, 1955), p. 31.

4. See Reinhold Niebuhr, *Love and Justice: Selections from the Shorter Writings of Reinhold Niebuhr,* ed. by D. B. Robertson (Cleveland: World Publishing Co., 1967).

5. T. S. Eliot, "Four Quartets: Little Gidding," *The Complete Poems and Plays 1909–1950* (New York: Harcourt, Brace & Co., 1952), p. 142.

6. Reinhold Niebuhr, *The Irony of American History* (New York: Charles Scribner's Sons, 1952), esp. pp. vii–viii.

7. H. E. W. Turner, *The Patristic Doctrine of Redemption* (London: A. R. Mowbray & Co., 1952); Sydney Cave, *The Doctrine of the Work of Christ* (London: University of London Press, 1959); F. W. Dillistone, *The Christian Understanding of Atonement* (Philadelphia: Westminster Press, 1968); Leonard Hodgson, *The Doctrine of the Atonement* (London: Nisbet & Co., 1951).

8. Calvin, Commentary on Acts 19:23.

9. Calvin, *Institutes* 3.6.3.

10. See Turner, pp. 53ff.

11. Jaroslav Pelikan, *The Christian Tradition: A History of the Development of Doctrine,* vol. 1, *The Emergence of the Catholic Tradition (100–600)* (Chicago: University of Chicago Press, 1971), p. 148.

12. Turner, ch. 4; Pelikan, pp. 232ff.

13. Cf. Donald M. Baillie, *God Was in Christ: An Essay on Incarnation and Atonement* (New York: Charles Scribner's Sons, 1948), esp. chs. 7 and 8.

14. Robert L. Calhoun's class lectures at Yale University on the History of Christian Doctrine.

15. H. R. Mackintosh, *The Christian Experience of Forgiveness* (London: Nisbet & Co., 1947), pp. 187, 234.

16. George Bernard Shaw, as quoted by Mackintosh in *The Christian Experience of Forgiveness,* p. 211.

17. Peter Abailard: *Exposition of the Epistle to the Romans,* in *A Scholastic Miscellany: Anselm to Ockham,* ed. and tr. by Eugene R. Fairweather, LCC (Philadelphia: Westminster Press, 1956), pp. 283–284.

18. Karl Barth, *Church Dogmatics* (Edinburgh: T. & T. Clark, 1956), vol. IV/1, pp. 351–352.

19. Ibid., p. 341; cf. Thomas Torrance: "The Christian doctrine of the resurrection cannot do without its empirical correlate in the empty tomb;

cut that away and it becomes non-sensical" (*Space, Time, and Incarnation* [London: Oxford University Press, 1969], p. 90).

20. Barth, *Church Dogmatics,* vol. IV/1, p. 336.

21. Rodion Shchedrin, *Lenin in the People's Heart* (Moscow, 1972), pp. 25–32.

22. Martin Niemöller, *Here I Stand* (Chicago: Willett, Clark & Co., 1937), pp. 150–155.

23. Paul Tillich, "Existentialist Aspects of Modern Art," *Christianity and the Existentialists,* ed. by Carl Michalson (New York: Charles Scribner's Sons, 1956), p. 143.

Chapter 4: God's Providing, Ordering, and Caring

1. John Calvin, *Institutes of the Christian Religion* 1.16.1.

2. Augustine, *City of God,* book 1, tr. by Henry Bettenson, intro. by David Knowles (New York: Penguin Books, 1981).

3. Herbert Butterfield, *Writings on Christianity and History,* ed. by C. T. McIntyre (New York: Oxford University Press, 1979), p. 3.

4. Calvin, *Institutes* 1.16.2, 5, 7.

5. Albert C. Outler, *Who Trusts in God: Musings on the Meaning of Providence* (New York: Oxford University Press, 1968); cf. Austin Farrer, *Love Almighty and Ills Unlimited: An Essay on Providence and Evil* (Garden City, N.Y.: Doubleday & Co., 1961).

6. George Arthur Buttrick, *Prayer* (Nashville: Abingdon-Cokesbury Press, 1952), p. 93; G. K. Chesterton, as found in Sherwood Eliot Wirt and Kersten Beckstrom, eds., *Living Quotations for Christians* (New York: Harper & Row, 1974), p. 92.

7. See Matthew Arnold's prose translation, "Thanksgiving of St. Francis for All Created Things, Usually Called the Canticle of the Sun," H. Martin P. Davidson, *Good Christian Men* (New York: Charles Scribner's Sons, 1940), p. 125.

8. Nathaniel Micklem, *Ultimate Questions* (Nashville: Abingdon Press, 1955), p. 57.

9. Karl Barth, *Church Dogmatics* (Edinburgh: T. & T. Clark, 1956), vol. III/3, p. 288.

10. Ian Barbour, *Issues in Science and Religion* (Englewood Cliffs, N.J.: Prentice-Hall, 1966), pp. 419ff.

11. Calvin, *Institutes* 1.16.5, 7.

12. John Dillenberger, *Protestant Thought and Natural Science: A Historical Interpretation* (Garden City, N.Y.: Doubleday & Co., 1960), ch. 4.

13. William Temple, *Nature, Man, and God* (London: Macmillan & Co., 1940), pp. 283–384.

14. Ibid., p. 267.

15. Harry Emerson Fosdick, "Will Science Displace God?", in *Adventurous Religion and Other Essays* (London: SCM Press, 1926), pp. 135–151.

16. William Temple, *Christus Veritas* (London: Macmillan & Co., 1949), pp. 193–198.

17. Cf. Reinhold Niebuhr's sermon on "The Providence of God" in *Justice and Mercy*, ed. by Ursula M. Niebuhr (New York: Harper & Row, 1974), pp. 14ff.

18. Westminster Shorter Catechism, Question 1.

19. John Hick, *Evil and the God of Love* (London: Macmillan Publishers, 1977).

20. Augustine, *Enchiridion* 8.23.

21. Augustine, *City of God* 4.11.

22. Irenaeus, *Proof of the Apostolic Preaching*, ch. 12 in *Ancient Christian Writers*, tr. by Joseph P. Smith (London: Longmans Green & Co., 1952); Irenaeus, *Against Heresies*, 4.39.1, *The Ante-Nicene Fathers* (Buffalo, N.Y.: Christian Literature Co., 1885–1887), vol. 1.

23. John Calvin, *Letters of John Calvin*, ed. by Jules Bonnet (Philadelphia: Presbyterian Board of Publication, 1858).

24. Butterfield, *Writings on Christianity and History*, p. 8.

25. Ibid., pp. 10–11.

26. Ibid., p. 11.

Chapter 5: Chosen Before the Foundation of the World

1. Jacques Monod, *Chance and Necessity* (New York: William Collins Sons & Co., 1972), pp. 160–161.

2. Arthur Koestler, *Darkness at Noon* (New York: Macmillan Co., Signet Books, 1953), p. 182.

3. Paul Johnson, *Modern Times: The World from the Twenties to the Eighties* (New York: Harper & Row, 1983), pp. 199ff., 413ff., 657, 516, 513ff., 533ff.

4. T. S. Eliot, "Choruses from 'The Rock,'" *The Complete Poems and Plays 1909–1950* (New York: Harcourt, Brace & Co., 1952), p. 103.

5. Nicholas Berdyaev, *The End of Our Time* (New York: Sheed & Ward, 1933), p. 54.

6. T. S. Eliot, *Complete Poems and Plays*, p. 196.

7. Augustine, *On the Profit of Believing*, in Philip Schaff, ed., *A Select Library of the Nicene and Post-Nicene Fathers of the Christian Church*, First Series, vol. III (Buffalo, N.Y.: Christian Literature Co., 1887), pp. 357–358.

8. Christopher Fry, *The Dark Is Light Enough* (London: Oxford University Press, 1954), p. 99, emphasis added. Used by permission of the publisher.

9. William Temple, *Christian Faith and Life* (London: SCM Press, 1950), ch. 6.

10. Paul Scherer, *For We Have This Treasure* (New York: Harper & Brothers, 1944), p. 131.

11. Karl Barth, *Church Dogmatics* (Edinburgh: T. & T. Clark, 1956), vol. IV/1, pp. 621ff.; vol. IV/2, pp. 584ff.

12. John Calvin, *Institutes of the Christian Religion* 3.10.6.

13. Barth, *Church Dogmatics*, vol. IV/1, p. 648.

14. Daniel Day Williams, *God's Grace and Man's Hope* (New York: Harper & Brothers, 1949), esp. ch. 8.

15. "The good and the righteous fight their way into Paradise over the corpses of their neighbors, less good and righteous than themselves." Nicholas Berdyaev, *The Destiny of Man* (London: Geoffrey Bles, Centenary Press, 1945), p. 114.

16. A. A. Hodge, *Outlines of Theology* (New York: A. C. Armstrong & Son, 1897), chs. 15–16.

17. Walter Lowrie, "Easter Only Once a Year," *Theology Today,* vol. 9, no. 1, p. 102.

18. From a personal letter to the writer dated February 6, 1986.

19. William Temple, *Nature, Man, and God* (London: Macmillan & Co., 1940), p. 452.

20. Austin Farrer, *A Celebration of Faith* (London: Hodder & Stoughton, 1970), p. 165.

21. Paul Tillich, "The World Situation," in Henry P. van Dusen, ed., *The Christian Answer* (New York: Charles Scribner's Sons, 1945), p. 10.

22. Leon Wencelius, *Calvin et Rembrandt* (Paris: Société d'Edition "Les Belles Lettres," n.d.), pp. 85–86.

Chapter 6: A New Heaven and a New Earth

1. Tony Rothman, "This Is the Way the World Ends," in *Discover,* vol. 8, no. 7 (July 1987), pp. 82–93.

2. "Armageddon theology, as we know it today, originated with Hal Lindsey, author of *The Late Great Planet Earth* (1970). His books have sold twenty and thirty million copies, making him the best-selling author of the 1970's" (G. Clarke Chapman, Jr., "Falling in Rapture Before the Bomb," in *The Reformed Journal,* vol. 37, no. 6 [June 1987], p. 12).

3. T. S. Eliot, "The Hollow Men," *The Complete Poems and Plays 1909–1950* (New York: Harcourt, Brace & Co., 1952), p. 59.

4. W. B. Yeats, *The Complete Poems of W. B. Yeats* (New York: Macmillan Co., 1973), pp. 184–185; cf. B. L. Reid, *William Butler Yeats, the Lyric of Tragedy* (Norman, Okla.: University of Oklahoma Press, 1961), p. 136.

5. Robert Browning, *Asolando,* Epilogue, st. 3; cf. Hugh Martin, *The Faith of Robert Browning* (London: SCM Press, 1963), pp. 104–105.

6. Peter Brown, *Augustine of Hippo, a Biography* (London: Faber & Faber, 1967), ch. 27.

7. *Early Christian Fathers,* tr. and ed. by Cyril C. Richardson, LCC (Philadelphia: Westminster Press, 1953), pp. 216–217.

8. John H. S. Burleigh, *The City of God: A Study of Augustine's Philosophy* (London: Nisbet & Co. 1949), pp. 23ff.; Charles N. Cochrane, *Christianity and Classical Culture: A Study of Thought and Action from Augustus to Augustine* (New York: Oxford University Press, 1957), ch. 10.

9. Augustine, *Expositions on the Book of Psalms,* ed. by A. Cleveland Coxe, in Philip Schaff, ed., *A Select Library of the Nicene and Post-Nicene Fathers of the Christian Church,* First Series, vol. VIII (Buffalo, N.Y.: Christian Literature Co., 1888), p. 678; R. A. Markus, *Saeculum: History and Society in the*

Theology of St. Augustine (Cambridge: Cambridge University Press, 1970), p. 30.

10. Augustine, *City of God* 19.17, tr. by Henry Bettenson (Baltimore: Penguin Books, 1972), pp. 877–879.

11. An address of Emil Brunner at Yale University Divinity School as remembered by the writer.

12. Reinhold Niebuhr, *The Nature and Destiny of Man* (New York: Charles Scribner's Sons, 1941, 1943), vol. 2, pp. 68ff.

13. Christian realism has been expounded by Reinhold Niebuhr with a brilliance found in no other work. His Gifford Lectures, *The Nature and Destiny of Man*, attempted to answer the question of the limits and the possibilities of history.

Niebuhr's thought has been expounded with great competence in two essays by Langdon Gilkey, "Reinhold Niebuhr as a Political Theologian" in *Reinhold Niebuhr and the Issues of Our Time*, ed. by Richard Harries (Oxford: A. R. Mowbray & Co., 1986), pp. 157–182, and "Reinhold Niebuhr's Theology of History" in *Journal of Religion,* vol. 54, no. 4 (October 1974). In the latter essay, Gilkey contrasts Niebuhr's thought with liberation theology.

14. Augustine, *Confessions* 1.1, in *Augustine: Confessions and Enchiridion,* tr. and ed. by Albert C. Outler, LCC (Philadelphia: Westminster Press, 1955), p. 31.

15. Reinhold Niebuhr, *Moral Man and Immoral Society* (New York: Charles Scribner's Sons, 1932), p. 22.

16. Reinhold Niebuhr, "Christian Faith and Social Action," in John Hutchison, ed., *Christian Faith and Social Action* (New York: Charles Scribner's Sons, 1953), p. 240.

17. Herbert Butterfield, *Writings in Christianity and History*, p. 167: "Three things, however, seem to illustrate the importance of Christianity in that mundane history which is under discussion—the importance of the particular religion which presided over the rise of what we call our Western civilisation. They all spring from the very nature of the Christian gospel itself and their effects on our civilisation are merely the incidental results of the ordinary religious activity of the Church—they are not a sample or a vindication of the mundane policies of ecclesiastics. They are by-products of the missionary and spiritual work of the Church, and it is not clear that the same mundane benefits would accrue if men set out with the object of procuring the mundane benefits—if men worked with their eyes on the by-products themselves. They show that the Church has best served civilisation not on the occasions when it had civilisation as its conscious object, but when it was most intent on the salvation of souls and most content to leave the rest to Providence. The three things are the leavening effect of Christian charity, the assertion of the autonomy of spiritual principle, and the insistence on the spiritual character of personality. Apart from the softening effect that religion often (but perhaps not always) has had on manners and morals, these

things have had their influences on the very texture of our Western civilisation."

18. Arnold Toynbee spoke of an increase in the means of grace in a Sherwood Eddy seminar at Toynbee Hall, London, in July 1951, in answer to a question about progress, according to the memory of the writer.

19. A. D. Lindsay, *The Two Moralities: Our Duty to God and to Society* (London: Eyre & Spottiswoode, 1940), p. 49.

20. Stanley Hauerwas, *Character and the Christian Life* (San Antonio: Trinity University Press, 1975), p. 233.

21. Kenneth Scott Latourette, *The History of the Expansion of Christianity* (New York: Harper & Brothers, 1945), vol. 3, p. 399.

22. Claus Westermann, *Genesis 1–11: A Commentary,* tr. by John J. Scullion (Minneapolis: Augsburg Publishing House, 1984), pp. 472–477.

23. *Reformed Witness Today: A Collection of Confessions and Statements of Faith Issued by Reformed Churches,* ed. by Lukas Vischer (Evangelische Arbeitsstelle Oekumene Schweiz, 1982), pp. 147–149.

24. Personal conversation with the writer.

Chapter 7: The Presence and the Power of God

1. Karl Barth, *Church Dogmatics,* vol. IV/1 (Edinburgh: T. & T. Clark, 1956), pp. 650ff.; vol. IV/3, pp. 109ff.

2. John Calvin, *Institution of the Christian Religion* (1536 edition of the *Institutes*), tr. and annotated by Ford Lewis Battles (Atlanta: John Knox Press, 1975), p. 80.

3. C. F. D. Moule, *The Holy Spirit* (Grand Rapids: Wm. B. Eerdmans Publishing Co., 1978), p. 74.

4. See Albert C. Outler, *The Rule of Grace* (Melbourne: United Church Press, 1982), pp. 9ff.

5. Barth, *Church Dogmatics,* vol. IV/1, p. 646.

6. John V. Taylor, *The Go-Between God: The Holy Spirit and the Christian Mission* (Philadelphia: Fortress Press, 1972), pp. 7ff.

7. Barth, *Church Dogmatics,* vol. IV/1, p. 648.

8. John Calvin, *Institutes of the Christian Religion* 1.9.1–3.

9. Albert C. Outler, *The Christian Tradition and the Unity We Seek* (New York: Oxford University Press, 1957), pp. 66, 54.

10. Ibid., pp. 110–112.

11. See *Institutes of the Christian Religion* 3.3.16–17. Calvin obviously placed emphasis on gathering for worship and on a routine of prayer (e.g., 2.8.30–34; 3.20.50). He insisted on the reading of the Bible insofar as this was practical in a day of low literacy and scarcity of Bibles. Yet he did not advocate religious exercises, apparently for three reasons: (1) the danger of confusing the exercise with the reality of the heart; (2) the danger of introspection, concentrating the attention on the self; (3) the practices of life in the congregation appointed by the New Testament, based on Acts 2:42, were all that is needed.

12. John E. Smith, *Experience and God* (New York: Oxford University Press, 1968), p. 71.

13. See the excellent discussion of the means of grace in Hendrikus Berkhof, *Christian Faith: An Introduction to the Study of the Faith,* rev. ed. (Grand Rapids: Wm. B. Eerdmans Publishing Co., 1985), pp. 349–397.

14. Steven Ozment, *The Age of Reform: An Intellectual and Religious History of Late Medieval and Reformation Europe* (New Haven, Conn.: Yale University Press, 1980), pp. 202–203.

15. Barth, *Church Dogmatics,* vol. IV/2, p. 640.